Flying Grounded

Flying Grounded

✦

My Spiritual Triumph Over Female Bullying

Tami McCandlish

iUniverse, Inc.

New York Lincoln Shanghai

Flying Grounded
My Spiritual Triumph Over Female Bullying

iUniverse books may be ordered through booksellers or by contacting:

iUniverse
2021 Pine Lake Road, Suite 100
Lincoln, NE 68512
www.iuniverse.com
1-800-Authors (1-800-288-4677)

ISBN: 978-0-595-45839-4 (pbk)
ISBN: 978-0-595-69713-7 (cloth)
ISBN: 978-0-595-90140-1 (ebk)

Printed in the United States of America

To my Savior, Jesus Christ.
And
To Mom, Dad, Mattie, and Charlie.
Thank you for your patience, support, acceptance, and love, especially during the time
that I spent writing this book.
I cherish each of you.

Author's Note

This book is based on my personal experience with bullying. In order to protect my characters' identities and honor their privacy, names and potentially revealing details have been changed. This is with exception to referenced professionals and Russ Clear, who has granted written permission to use his name. My writing does not represent the ideas or opinions of my family, friends, or acquaintances. This book is not intended to be a record of wrongs but as an insightful, inspirational work that challenges readers to evaluate their relational experiences, raise their standards of compassion, and explore their faith.

Contents

Introduction

"Shhhhhhh ... Tryin' tuh watch my shooowah!" snaps my teenage sister while engrossed in a Tivoed episode of MTV's recent reality show *Laguna Beach.*

Like duh, what was I thinkin' being all noisy? She's a diehard. She doesn't miss an episode. She *can't* be interrupted. She and our cousin even nicknamed themselves after the characters, and they are not the only ones. Each season, my sis, along with millions of other teen and young adult viewers, is captivated by a handful of wealthy, Californian teenage girls who, over the course of the school year, duke-it-out in the name of boys, beauty, and popularity.[1]

I hated the show so much its first season that I refused to watch it. All it took was one episode—the first episode—to bring back that haunting queasiness. What turned me off—the potent rivalry—was the same thing that drew in so many other viewers. I did not want to be reminded of how cruel girls could be, and I did not want to see them secretively and underhandedly compete against each other. Nevertheless, during season two, I finally caved and decided to let myself in on the craze of *Laguna* in hopes of learning about the girls and how they worked through their problems.

Careful not to sound too interested and trying my best to act as if I were still annoyed by the show, I interrupted my sister again and asked, "What are *those* girls up to now?" The T.V. paused, and I got a typical teenage not-right-now, raised eyebrow look.

"Okay," I said. "Sorry I asked."

I opened up the fridge and pretended to look for a snack, but I could not resist listening in to yet another episode in which many of the *Laguna* girls did all the things that I had seen ordinary girls do to each other before.

In their social circles, the *Laguna* girls dished out harsh critiques, inconspicuous dirty looks and whispers, snide remarks, and mocking laughs. They would single-out a particular girl (sometimes a friend, other times an enemy) and say things like, "I hate her. I wish she'd get out of my life," or, "I can't stand to listen to her voice ... She's *so* annoying," or, "She's *so* fake ... *So* stupid ... *So* immature." They called other girls "bitches," "'ho's," "sluts," and "whores," and they verbally attacked other girls for things like clothes, hairstyles, and boyfriends. On the surface, the reasons for the attacks seemed petty, and every time I saw another girl become wounded by this behavior, my heart tearfully twisted. Oftentimes, the targeted girls seemed powerless. Many of them refrained from confrontation or ignored the attacks and hid their true emotions from friends and family. Some of the girls disconnected from friends, boyfriends, and socializing in general, and some of them even lost boyfriends and long-time friends due to the mean girls' manipulative, destructive actions.

With each new season of *Laguna,* which is now *Newport Harbor,* the alliances and rivalries seem to grow bigger, badder, and much more hurtful. It appears that each new group of girls learns the basics as underclassmen and, once they become upperclassmen, they adopt an even more intense policy of underground meanness. A portion of me just does not get why they constantly turn petty issues into full-blown psychological combat. However, more of me *totally* gets why they constantly turn petty issues into full-blown psychological combat. I know exactly what they are going through. I have been there, through all of the same kind of issues, and because of this I desperately desire to intervene in the damage happening between the girls on MTV and between many other girls and women in general.

True, these shows have their moments in which they beautifully highlight the strength in female friendships, but those moments are usually overshadowed by countless instances where the battle between two girls or two groups of girls has less to do with party invites, hookups, and $600 slingbacks and everything to do with being generally trumped by each other.[2]

Plenty of other popular shows' storylines revolve around *Laguna*-like social damage created by toxic rivalry and secretive communication. I constantly notice it on many MTV shows like *The Real World, Road Rules, The Hills, My Super Sweet Sixteen,* and I also notice it on other networks' shows like *Big Brother, Survivor, The Bachelor, The Apprentice, The Amazing Race, America's Next Top Model, The Surreal Life, The Ultimate Coyote Ugly Search, Desperate Housewives, Access Hollywood,* each and every soap opera, and the list goes on and on and on.

Even if you do not watch much T.V., I bet you have seen this type of behavior elsewhere. You have probably heard about it in classic fairytales like Cinderella, read it in literature like Margaret Atwood's *Cat's Eye,* watched it in plays and movies like *Les Miserables* and *Heathers,* listened to it in chart-topping pop and country songs like Avril Lavigne's "Girlfriend," Saving Jane's "Girl Next Door" and Lee Ann Womack's "I'll Think of a Reason Later," and you might have seen it posted on social networking websites such as MySpace and Facebook. We are surrounded by this type of behavior. And chances are most of us have been affected by it in our lives, at least to some extent and in some way.

In our lives, there have been times that we have felt that awful feeling that comes with being ganged up on, backstabbed, unnecessarily criticized, wrongly accused, and called bad names. We have felt the rejection and exclusion that accompanies our peers' unwelcoming silence and cold stares. Some of us have been ticked off at others so badly that, like the *Laguna* girls, we and/or our friends have done some backbiting, bad-mouthing, rumor spreading, or evil-eye casting. Some of us have just observed the behavior from those around us and choose to stay out of things. If you are a female you especially know what I mean. I have talked to plenty of you that say, "That has happened to me!" or you ask, "Why are girls/women so mean?" or you simply start telling your story before I have had the chance to tell you mine.

Regardless of whether you are on the receiving, giving, or observing end of this type of conduct, the results of this behavior can forever imprint our lives. Studies show that it can lead to "higher incidences of depression, school drop-outs, substance abuse, early parenthood, delinquency and criminal behavior," as well as Post Traumatic Stress Disorder, and self-inflicted abuse such as eating disorders, cutting, or suicide.[3]

Yet, aside from the potentially harmful effects, our culture glamorizes, eroticizes, and marginalizes this treatment by playfully and misleadingly naming it "drama," "entertainment," and "catfighting." In doing so, we set-up a stage, dim the lights, engage the actors, and close the curtains on a common emotional and psychological form of bullying called relational aggression, also known as female bullying.[4]

Relational aggression is what author Natalie Angier in *Woman: An Intimate Geography* says to be like "a voodoo hex, an anonymous but obsessive act in which the antagonist's soul, more than her body, must be got at, must be penetrated, must be nullified."[5] This covert aggression might seem relatively minor to some people, but oftentimes the damage done is major.

Relational aggression occurs when a network of friends deliberately use indirect tactics such as rumors, teasing, name-calling, dirty looks, the silent treatment, whispering, talking-behind-the-back, betrayal, exclusion, and intimidation, among other behaviors, to target and alienate a person that has posed some kind of trouble, threat, or competition to the alliance. This is all done with the intent to eliminate the target as a problem, which often results in the target's confidence and reputation being blemished or destroyed.[6]

Many researchers link this form of bullying to middle school, junior high, and high school girls, because it is during these periods that relational aggression spikes dramatically due to the great significance placed on relationships.[7] I remember a multitude of relationally aggressive episodes in my youth, and whenever I asked adults why girls were so mean, I heard, "That's just how girls are ... jealous." Yet, as much as we like to think that this is strictly a jealous teenage girl problem, it is not.

Numerous studies show that females, more than males, tend to use relational aggression to control their social spheres. However, passive aggression can be dished out and felt by *anyone*, regardless of a person's age, gender, race, status, or personal background. From children to adults, males to females, the powerful to the powerless, we can all be affected in any social environment, from primary and secondary schools to colleges, businesses, churches, dating and familial settings, and on the Internet.[8]

Ultimately, relational aggression is an issue that affects a wide range of people in a variety of situations. Nevertheless, this form of aggression is generally and routinely applied to females because our society reinforces the rationalization that this behavior is a traditional, natural practice—a rite of passage—among girls and women. As a result, this all-too convenient, overused excuse fails to dig down into the muck of this crisis and deal with the issues at hand. As a society, if we are to fully understand relational aggression, we must first take a look at the underlying causes, because once we better understand why this happens, we can produce a healthier, higher standard of social representation for females.[9]

As girls and women, it is largely our responsibility to break this socialization and demand that other people follow our action. In the last 30 years, we have successfully altered other ways in which we are perceived. We have come a long way and continue to make great strides in achieving equality with males, as we have found increasing opportunity and empowerment through sports, politics, and employment.[10] And it is in these areas that our competitiveness is most likely complimented.

For example, in most sports, we can come pretty close to openly expressing our need to dominate and win. We can physically go-at-it in order to get the ball. We can show anger, stomp, scream, and shout—as long as it is all done to bring prestige to our teams and institutions.

However, when we walk out of the sports arena and into the pressure of our everyday social lives and intimate relationships, we are not permitted to convey the same type of behaviors and emotions. If we go after anything that we want for ourselves—peer admiration, a male, a job title, or anything of the like—we will be labeled intolerable, jealous, and bitchy and will be shunned by our peers. According to Kate Fillion, author of *Lip Service: The Truth About Women's Darker Side in Love, Sex, and Friendship*, it is here that "competition tends to be viewed as a force for harm" because a girl or woman who is socially competitive "appears to be trying to break away from other [girls or] women and assert that she is different—better, in fact. She seeks recognition for herself alone, and plays to win without seeming to mind that her own victory may entail someone else's defeat." Socially, being competitive turns into "a criticism that implies serious transgression: wanting too much for oneself, and caring too little about others."[11]

As girls and women, we are expected to be walking, talking, Hallmark cards. We are always thought to be emotionally in-touch with each of our relationships. Our society expects us to be nurturing, charming, charitable, empathetic, and non-confrontational. It tells us that we cannot disagree about anything and that we must see to it that none of us get separated, overshadowed, or hurt.[12] At the same time that our society depicts us as superhero caretakers, it also stereotypes us as catty, mean, selfish, and deceitful. Both depictions create great difficulty when it comes to directly dealing with the disagreements and rivalries that arise in our lives.[13]

The task of fulfilling this assignment can be very confusing because it conveys a distorted message about society's expectations of us and how and where it is acceptable for us to vent emotion. Instead of telling us that it is natural to be imperfect, angry, envious, competitive, and scared and teaching us ways to productively articulate and manage those emotions, our culture leaves us with the complicated dilemma of figuring out how to balance both a conventional and a modern identity, or as author Nan Mooney puts it, "looking clean while dealing dirty."[14] We have no choice but to figure out how to silently assert ourselves by turning healthy competition into toxic rivalry. Because of this inconsistency, we are forced into unhealthy character development, which includes self-depreciation, dishonesty, dependency, envy, rivalry, and hatred, and we are permitted, throughout our lives, to take our aggression out on each other indirectly and secretively rather than on our culture at large.[15] Until we strike a reasonable balance between competition and cooperation, and until we model that balance and teach it to younger generations, we will never reach the relational levels we are capable of attaining.[16]

As females, we play a vital role in facilitating positive change. If we are to prevent this harmful behavior, it is imperative that we reinvent our definition of aggression. We *must* name and acknowledge relational bullying as a problem, and we *must* come to terms with our involvement, whether it is as bullies, victims, bully-victims, bystanders, or a mix of all roles.[17] Too often, when we notice the personal relevance of this issue, we become defensive or deny our participation out of fear of condemnation, because we have been taught that confrontation is negative and that girls and women who directly confront others are failures of femininity.[18] If we never learn to be comfortable with conflict and confrontation, we will always have difficulty deciphering normal disagreements from personal attacks and betrayals, and we will never develop and sustain the incredible friendships and relationships that we so deserve.[19] Failing to acknowledge and talk about the seriousness of relational aggression, the reasons behind it, and our participation in it, preserves its destructiveness and promotes its reoccurrence.

While writing this book, it was extremely difficult for me to come to terms with my own roles with relational bullying. Throughout my adolescence, I strived to be that sweet, virtuous All-American cover-girl, but that was not always who I was.

As a schoolgirl, I remember several times that I got caught-up in the recess, lunch table, and locker room I-can't-believe-she-did-that details and the she-said-they-said accusations. While it was meaningful to have a group of people to release aggressive feelings to, I am regretful to have partaken in moments of harsh criticism, resentment, gossip, and even physical retaliation toward my peers, because I now know the harm relational aggression can bring.

My most memorable encounters with relational aggression occurred in middle school and persisted throughout junior high, high school, college, and my careers. However, it was in high school that I underwent severe victimization. Even as a smart, confident, involved student-athlete that always had a boyfriend and had friends galore, I was wounded so badly that I felt the only way to escape my hurt would be to end my existence.

During this project, I became convinced that males are just as capable of employing indirect aggression as females. I have heard stories about alliance building among boys in athletics, and I have witnessed how slander, backstabbing, and betrayal from men have deeply affected other men in the business world. In reflecting upon my experience, I see that boys and men were heavily involved in my situation (especially when the reward was female admiration). However, I believe my experience to be female-rooted. Therefore, the subsequent chapters will primarily focus on female-oriented bullying. That is not to say that I am only addressing female readers, though. In knowing that this is a subject that males become involved with directly and indirectly through their own lives as well as their wives, girlfriends, sisters, daughters, and friends, I write to the opposite sex as well.

My story is not the typical victim-of-bullying story that is so often depicted in the media. You will see that I was not the weak, rejected girl targeted only by the strong, powerful cheerleaders and jocks. My circumstance was one in which my happiness, strengths, achievements, and respected status was stomped on and destroyed not just by those that held social power but also by those who did not.

During high school, my perpetrators seemed unstoppable. No one, not my parents, school counselors or administrators, attorneys, or law enforcement officers knew how to halt my offenders' injurious behaviors. The lack of helpful solutions and support, made me feel disregarded and dispirited, and I saw no choice but to abide by the only suggestions given to me—to pretend to get over it and ignore my bullies. However, my silence did not lessen the conflict; it only escalated it.

My attempt to ignore this abuse caused me to suppress anger that I direly needed to release, and it motivated my bullies to attack me full-force with dirty looks, rumors, insults, threats, and physical assaults. Because the regularity of my bullies' actions made me feel unsafe and made me fear the ruin of my reputation, I attempted to save myself by becoming a reactive aggressor. Consequently, I was ridiculed, ostracized, and humiliated by my peer community, which led to years of personal inner struggle. As a result, not only did I disown everything and every person affiliated with my school and hometown, but I also attempted to fend off my entire gender by avoiding interaction with females.

It was during college, when I once again became the target of relational aggression, that I uprooted my dormant Christian faith and regained my mental, physical, and emotional well-being. After months of regular spiritual meditation, I found my most effective coping mechanism to be the death and resurrection of Jesus Christ. It was through Him that I discovered that someone knew relational bullying just as well as I did, and it was through His Spirit that I was called to re-evaluate my perception of females and gain hope for future relationships with them.

However, even after faith brought me peace and healing, my lack of education about relational aggression left me incapable of speaking out against it. It was not until a month after I graduated from college, when I happened upon journalist Rachel Simmons' book *Odd Girl Out: The Hidden Culture of Aggression in Girls*, that I was able to fully validate my experience. My parents had purchased the book for our family shortly after my last year of high school. At the time, because I was still blinded by hurt and rage, I stuffed the book away in the clutter of our hutch, convinced that no one had a clue as to what I had been through. Four years later, after my spiritual healing, I rediscovered the book and started reading, and my experience was further authenticated.

I am enormously grateful for Simmons' work and the work that many other professionals have brought to surface regarding this topic. These individuals have defined my experience, given me voice, showed me that I was not alone, and provided me with inspiration to fight this problem. With the aid of their research, it is my intention to bring other girls and women a personal, familiar account in which they can draw from so that they too can explore, write, and talk about their own stories. From the accounts that have been brought to my attention, I know that so many other girls and women have at least one story, no matter how insignificant they think it may be.

I understand this is a delicate, forbidden subject to many people. I understand my boldness and bluntness places me in a dangerous situation, as in telling what I believe to be the truth challenges the societal norm. While I certainly do not expect all of my readers to agree with how I have told my story, I pray that they will read this work constructively, with the understanding that relational aggression is an issue that affects countless people, not just a select few. The words I have used, the emotions I express, the issues I bring forth are not candy-coated. They are real. They are raw. They do not just represent my frustration but also the frustration of many other girls and women.

If you find offense in my unromantic portrayals please understand this is not an attack on girls or women. I realize that there are times in my writing that I reinforce stereotypes. I do this because, in my past, sexist labels were all I knew to believe and they were the easiest excuses to apply to my problems. However, I no longer stand behind such generalizations. Therefore, it is the stereotypes that I am attacking in hopes to bring more awareness about them so that we can use them to examine the underlying causes for the problems we experience.

Neither is the depiction of my characters meant to be an attack but a call to all of us for improvement. My characters were not bad people. I believe some of them to have been strong, determined individuals, others lost souls who longed for acceptance, all potential leaders. Unfortunately, they were not led to avenues that allowed them to engage and channel their feelings and actions in ways that permitted healthy emotional release and social mistakes.

Together, my characters and I shared the struggle. I too have felt and still feel socially restricted, and because of that I have violated boundaries—theirs, mine, and others. It is through my story that I hope the characters of my past and I, along with other females and anyone who has played a part in relational bullying, experience positive shame in the damage we have done and continue to do to each other. It is also my hope that we can alter our circumstances by exploring how spiritual pathways can enhance our individual and group identities and bring fairness to our relationships.

Clique & Company

Before I begin my story, I would like to share the typical hierarchy of a female clique so that you will better understand my roles and actions, my characters' roles and actions, your roles and actions, and your peers' roles and actions. I am not attempting to associate my readers with particular roles. I do not know your situations, so I cannot make specific claims. However, I believe most of us can relate with the concept of a clique. Most of us have some kind of memory of cliques. Maybe our memories makes us hex those bigheaded Barbie and Ken cheerleaders and jocks who made us feel worthless in the hallways or cafeterias of our high schools, or maybe our memories make us feel instant denial. Whatever the reason for our reactions, 'clique' is a term that makes many of us cringe, because we generally associate it with meanness, exclusiveness, and bad popularity.[20] Not every clique or person within a clique is heartless and arrogant, though. Essentially, a clique is not an evil, life-sucking force, but any group of friends who share common interests and opinions.[21]

Clique formation is typical and can be beneficial. Building alliances allows us to embrace friendships, support, and advise one another through difficult experiences, privately release our frustrations, and increase our self-worth.[22] Cliques serve as a safety netting particularly for females, as females tend to "spend more time together, confide in one another more, and feel more trust in their friends than [males] do."[23] Unfortunately, relational aggression brings forth the dark side of cliques because far too often they are used to carry out hostility.[24]

Because of the overwhelming disapproval of cliques, females usually deny their involvement, but are quick to point-out other females' involvement. Even if females acknowledge their participation, they usually reject the facts that experts use to identify alliance formation, organization, and operation. Females will say that no one in the group is competitive or exclusive and that no one individual heads the group. Admitting to these things would be confessing to aggressiveness, the very characteristic that girls and women are instructed not to display. While acquaintanceship with cliques is often refuted, our society can no longer keep their negative behavior under-wraps, as studies have proven their recurrent destructiveness.[25]

1

Cliques are formed around a girl or woman who has everything that our society tells us is important for a woman to have—beauty, fame, male admiration, style, wealth, a bit of athleticism, or any other advantage that others have difficulty accessing. With these indispensable assets, a leader gets her peers to take her side and not her rival's.[26]

Once a clique is established, the female with central power acts as a CEO, managing her associates in a business-like fashion, keeping them in positions that assure they will not trade-out to an opponent or leave her solely responsible for her actions. To prevent her flaws from being revealed and to secure her members' loyalty, the leader offers her friends some kind of incentive.[27] For example, she might provide romance-incentive by saying something like, "My brother's best friends with your crush. If you want, I can tell him that you like him," or she might provide style-incentive by saying, "I really like your new shirt! I have a pair of boots that would match perfectly. You can sort through my entire wardrobe if you want," or, after a disagreement between two friends, she might offer support and protection to one of them by saying, "Just ignore her. She's a psycho. She hates our guts. You don't need her anyway."

When the leader's attempts to wheedle fail, her aggression really kicks-in. After she realizes a potential threat, she will attack. At first, she will casually share her dislike of her rival with her friends. Then, once everyone seems to agree with her feelings, she will show outward disgust toward the person. As a result, the rest of the clique mimics her behavior and treats the target badly too by doing things like whispering and snickering when the target enters a room or completely ignoring the target.[28]

Group members look highly upon and fear the leader's status and power. Therefore, members willingly follow the leader's actions, knowing that resisting her would likely result in social suicide. Not only do members participate in exclusive activities because it prevents them from being ridiculed, it also tightens the group's bond and gives them a sense of authority. Even if a girl is an outsider to the clique, she can increase her chances of being initiated into it by ditching her existing friends and harassing the target.[29]

Below is a description of a classic, Alpha girlhood alliance using the seven primary roles developed by Rosalind Wiseman in *Queen Bees and Wannabes: Helping Your Daughter Survive Cliques, Boyfriends, and Other Realities of Adolescence*.[30]

The chief member or leader of the clique is the **Queen Bee**. This female thrives on power and uses sex appeal, style, and brains to control her environment. She is usually known as the most popular girl in her grade, school, or social setting. In most cases, there are multiple Queen Bees within one environment.[31]

Many of her peers feel that challenging her superiority is off-limits and instead opt to bow to her wants and needs. This girl is a master at weakening her group members' friendships with those outside the clique and with those who pose a threat to the clique. If she feels threatened, be prepared for her if-you-diss-me-I-will-diss-you mentality, but do not expect her to admit when she hurts another person's feelings. She will not or she has great difficulty doing so.

Next in line is the **Sidekick**, the Queen Bee's best bud. She will back the Queen no matter what, because she is dependent on the confidence she gets from the throne. In copying the Queen Bee's fashion and mannerisms, she feels an undeniable bond that the two of them rein supreme over all other girls. Together, they are usually the first in their grade to become "boy crazy," and they are the first to start dating upperclassmen. Despite all the "perks," the Sidekick's infatuation with the Queen Bee can cause the Sidekick to forget that she can think and act for herself.

The most complex, secretive thinker of the group is the **Banker**. She creates drama by collecting information and giving it out at times that she feels will boost her worth within the group. She is a casual talker and easily gains others' trust because she is careful not to come-off as a gossip, but as a concerned friend who is only trying to connect. She tends to be everyone's friend because she hardly ever steps into the limelight of disagreements; rather she ducks out just when a fight intensifies. This girl is valuable to the group and is rarely excluded because she always has the scoop on everyone else. Because she is quiet and shy in the presence of adults, she is not often suspected of instigating.

The **Floater** is perhaps the most independent individual of the group. She hops back and forth between multiple cliques. She has a lot of command but does not implement it in a way that makes others feel that they are beneath her. A solid sense of self-respect keeps her from being pressured to conform to one particular group's standards. She stays away from conflict and works hard not to leave anyone out.

Then there is the **Torn Bystander** who often gets trapped in the heart of quarrels involving friends or groups of friends. This girl is always frazzled because she has to choose between sides and making the wrong decision could be detrimental to her status. Even though she knows the Queen Bee and Sidekicks' actions are harsh, she defends their ways because it gives her access to all the benefits that come with popularity. This girl has trouble telling her friends "no" and instead "goes along to get along."

There is also the **Pleaser/Wannabe/Messenger**, who lo-o-o-ves to gossip and is always the person in the middle of a clash. Whether she is a part of the clique or trying to work her way in, she will do anything to gain the adoration of the Queen Bee and Sidekick. The only way to sustain her position and confidence is to keep the leaders happy by executing their plans. If she fails or if she becomes annoyingly clingy, she will be ousted. This girl is so fearful of being rejected by the clique and so desperate to win its approval that she easily looses her sense of self.

Lastly, there is the **Target**. This person, in some way, has social importance.[32] She can be an individual within or outside the clique. Either way, she has somehow challenged the authority of someone within the alliance (usually the Queen Bee or Sidekick). Bombarded with filthy looks, slander, and rejection, she feels embarrassed, hurt, lonely, vulnerable, and unable to prevent the clique from ganging up on her. She feels no one will side with her (especially adults) and that no one will take effective action against her offenders. Her way of coping is to conceal her distress by eliminating people from her life before they can reject her from their lives.[33]

While these seven categories are common, they are not fixed in all circumstances. Occasionally, positions are switched-up (i.e., at the beginning of the school year or while a co-worker is on vacation). Sometimes members play multiple parts within their group and sometimes they serve a particular role in one group but another role in a different group. Wiseman's descriptions may apply a little or a lot to your situation. Keep in mind that clique structure occurs in a variety of social groups, and it can be complex when considering different age, economic, geographic, and racial factors. At least these basics can help you better identify the group dynamics of my characters and your own peers.[34]

My Flock

As a young adult riding shotgun in my parents' Dodge Ram pickup, I remembered just how much I liked staring out the passenger window. When I was little, I loved observing my surroundings. I always kept lookout for deer and hawks in roadside fields and trees. I watched clouds morph and cast shadows across endless acres of meadows. At night, I counted stars, and I especially liked peering into people's illuminated houses.

Back then, my car rides were easygoing and trouble-free. I never had to worry about paying attention and reacting to drunk or narcoleptic drivers drifting left to center or wannabe NASCAR stars passing on a double-yellow incline. Instead, I left all the concerns of driving to my parents, expecting them to keep me safe. On this ride, I placed that same childlike trust in Mom so I could once again enjoy the view of the countryside.

Finally able to take in one of the prettiest scenes on the route, I tried counting the calves that speckled a farm's vivid green pastures, but I lost count when a group of migrating geese entered the frame. They paralleled the road with a continuous flapping routine. I had always thought it was so easy for birds to fly, but while I watched them, I realized that if they didn't have the wind-force to constantly boost them, their flying was an exhausting task.

As the flock faded into the rolling hills, I was reminded of another delectation of my childhood, when I myself had devoted much effort to flying. In my room, I would balance on my bed's footboard, close my eyes, and contemplate weightlessness. When I would hop off, I would land with such force that my parents would think that I had fallen through the floor. When jumping off my bed didn't produce results, I would go for attempt number two in the living room. Standing on our granite fireplace, I would wave my arms vigorously and thrust myself upward. My meetings with the floor always brought out my temper. With carpet-burned knees and elbows, I would pound my fists, jump up, and stomp back for another try. One unsuccessful effort wasn't going to stop me from conquering this endeavor. Next, I tried leaping off our front porch only to end up with grass stains on my hands and thighs. I would spring off our pool's diving board, but every time I got soaked. I would even drag my bike to the top of a 60-foot hill, crouch into torpedo position, push off, and hope to build speeds fast enough for elevation. My strained neck, clinched teeth, buggy eyeballed takeoffs had to create a humorous spectacle, but my crash landings were enough to make any mother cringe. After all, landing is the most dangerous part of flying for humans and birds—too hard or too fast could cause serious injuries.[35]

Thankfully, I never ended up with any broken bones, just disappointment in realizing that my feet were stuck to the ground. If there were only a way that I could have stayed in the air for a little while, I would have been pleased ... Actually, that wouldn't have been enough. I would have wanted more hang-time.

I had inherited my determination to fly honestly. As a child, Mom had leaped out of trees, and once she almost jumped off the roof of her house. Dad also sought out flight by flinging himself off tops of hay bales. Their faces would also glow red when they were pulled to the ground time and time again.

Although the members of my family and I came to terms with our inability to fly, we never allowed gravity to put us in park for too long. We were adamant in our will to succeed at anything we set out to accomplish; an attribute that I feel eventually caused us to be rejected by much of our hometown.

We lived in a Midwestern backwoods community located at the edge of the Appalachian foothills. The closest village had two gas stations and no traffic lights, a feed mill, a butcher shop, and a bank. Growing up in this old-fashioned setting, I never knew many rich people. It was a blue-collar area where generations of residents worked in their barns and fields, at several of the large factories, out of an 18-wheeler, or at the county hospital.

I started childhood like everyone else I knew—simplistically. I wasn't spoiled with lavish Christmases or birthdays, and if it weren't for my grandparents I wouldn't have had much clothing. For several years, I lived in a single-wide trailer. My parents drove used cars. They were barely able to pay bills. They never stashed extra cash to spend on designer clothes, filet mignon, or the number one movie at the box office.

Mom and Dad had arduously worked paycheck-to-paycheck long before I was born, at jobs in which they could now write their own stories of being relationally and physically bullied. Mom had been employed since she was 15 as a hotel maid, a bakery clerk and decorator, and a server at a pool concession. As an assembly line worker, she had sawed wood to make drawers for kitchen and bathroom cabinets, and at another factory job she had operated a riveter and tested car ignitions. Dad had also had an array of occupations. He had worked at an insect exterminating business, a glass factory, a battery company, a hardware shop, and a sand molding company. He had also folded boxes at a paper mill, delivered tires, and sold and distributed wood burning stoves for his dad's business.

Just when it felt as if their constant, backbreaking labor would never let-up, an opportunity for relief came about. When I was four, Dad left his snow plowing and pothole filling job at the county department and took a sales position at a new local business, a charitable gaming distribution company.

Throughout my youth, the company grew larger structurally and financially, and it became one of our area's most distinguished corporations; and Dad, despite only having a high school diploma, became one of its most reputable employees. He went on to sell millions, and my parents were able to pay off their debt and save for our family's future. Eventually, Dad was offered and accepted an executive position, but as his status and authority within the company increased, along with his salary, it created resentment from peers toward him and our family.

Sometimes after he returned home from work or from a trip into town, I would hear him grumbling about encounters with co-workers or community members who had inaccurately evaluated our circumstances. It wasn't only from Dad that I constantly heard about us being critiqued. The negative remarks of some adults (or their children) were always within earshot.

"They don't deserve so much."
"They're taking *another* vacation!?"
"Those kids are *so* spoiled."
"They're *such* snobs."

Even during personal conversations, certain people would sarcastically say, "*You* can afford to buy it," or, "Must be nice to have *another* new car" (throughout the years Dad had received several company vehicles; all but one were pre-owned).[36]

All of the animosity seemed to result because of my parents' ability to capitalize on hardship and defy the financial regularity of our community. I never understood why people didn't want the best for my parents and family just as we did for them. Mom and Dad didn't give off a bow-down-to-us-because-we're-better-than-you vibe. They knew exactly how it felt to struggle and fail, and because of that, they gave physically and emotionally by befriending those who were depressed and frustrated with personal problems, by donating our outgrown clothes, by loaning money to friends who were in slumps, and by babysitting free of charge. Nonetheless, some of the people who they gladly helped chose to indirectly speak derogatorily about my parents and our family.

For the most part, my parents ignored being in the spotlight of beauty salon and PTO chatter. They usually didn't make too big of a deal about what people said, but when I overheard these types of things, it sparked a drive within me to show that my goodhearted, hardworking family *did* deserve the rewards we earned. Yet, it wasn't *just* my family's worthiness that I set out to prove.

Because I had been targeted as a result of my parents' successes, I began an individual quest to uphold my name against any kind of defamation. This ambition started in elementary school. When I received my Field Day ribbons—one blue, the rest red—I was thrilled to have placed in every event. However, when Zach Johnson and Jake Rosenberger, the cutest and most athletic boys in my class, laughed, and said that I wasn't good enough to get all blues, I cried. Prompted to never again allow any boy to joke about my shortcomings, I began using classroom and playground activities to gain respect.

The next year I upped my blue ribbon winnings, and when Zach and Jake saw my awards, they didn't laugh. Instead, they teased, "Not bad fur a *guuurrl*." They might as well have laughed at me again. Their comments launched me into an intense competition, in which I tried to show that my abilities were just as commendable, if not more, than theirs—than any boy's.

Sure, I played the occasional game of hopscotch and jump rope, but competing in male-dominated sports became my ultimate challenge. If in striving to win I swallowed half the dirt around home plate or took an elbow to the teeth underneath the basketball hoop, the pain was worth the rush that I got when I proved I could beat them.

In gym class, I showed that I was just as strong as all of the boys when I climbed to the top of the cargo net. At lunch, I scarfed down just as much pizza and chugged just as much chocolate milk as they did. In music class, I sang just as loudly as they sang. I beat them out of lead roles in plays. I got star stickers on my graded tests and made honor roll every quarter just like them. I broke through their Red Rover chains (or got clotheslined trying to do so). I ran from the blacktop to the fence just as quickly. I could kick a soccer ball just as far. Plus, at the end of the day, I always raced against them to claim the back seat of the bus.

Although I wasn't always victorious, these challenges just weren't satisfying enough. In forth grade, when I discovered that my girl friends were playing organized, co-ed basketball, it felt natural that I do the same so I could sustain my equivalency and dominance over my male opponents.

Game on.

Hoops and Halos

Basketball would eventually become my primary focus, but shortly after I began playing, I wanted to quit. Nowhere near instant success, I felt uncoordinated and debilitated. I cried when my coaches corrected my mistakes or when the boys took off dribbling down the court, leaving me lagging behind, bouncing the ball off my foot every couple of steps. Although, with weekly practices, I began to adapt, and within several demanding months of learning new techniques, receiving critiques, and adjusting to my role on the team, I actually started to like basketball.

Eventually, after a few years of being pressed by other players to perform at top-level, I became one of the league's most productive members on one of its most winning teams. When the girls' traveling coach attempted to recruit me, I refused to depart from little league ball. Even though the traveling league was considered "a step up" from the elementary league, playing traveling ball meant that I would have to participate on an all-girl team against all girls. The thought of making such a change made me feel like a sellout. Basketball wasn't about girls; it was about out-doing boys. Boys were "the other." Boys provided the hardest physical challenge. Boys were whom I was told I couldn't best. Prior to the Mia Hamm/Lisa Leslie/Gabrielle Reese, "We Got Next," girl-power era, society didn't expect me to defeat boys and if I did I was made to feel that I was doing something wrong.

Once, when I turned up my in-your-face defense and outshone my male opponent's stardom, his mom stormed down from the bleachers, claiming that I was deliberately trying to trip and punch her son. Now in this situation, I wasn't attempting to "take him out," but if a boy bodied up to me, I would body-up right back. That was the problem. The boys were supposed to overpower the little girls. Little girls weren't supposed to overpower the boys. Oddly, it was never the boys and hardly ever their dads who complained of my "vicious" play; rather it was their moms and sisters, who, to this day (sixteen years later), retell the "traumatic" events. As an adult, I now understand that to some female spectators, my wanting to attain more athletic achievement than the boys seemed to show a lack of humility and, in turn, a lack of ladylikeness. Nevertheless, as a child, I felt personally attacked and that feeling motivated me to press on in my efforts to defeat my male opponents. I *loved* beating the boys, and I wanted to do it forever, but as I approached junior high, the stage in which my school separated girls and boys in athletics, I realized that this pursuit would be made unattainable. I defied this same-sex segregation with all my might. Even so, I ended up surrendering to the division a year before I was required.

Because I wanted to participate in basketball all the time, I decided to play organized summer ball on an Amateur Athletic Union (AAU) team. In AAU, there were no co-ed teams, I had no choice but to join an all-girl squad and play against all girls too.

Considered to be the most advanced level, AAU was where ballers could play with the best, compete against the best, and be the best. As early as 12 and 13-years-old, players were already checking out big-name colleges, and big-name college coaches were already scoping the players out. Yet, with this highly competitive version of the game came intense issues. During an upswing of female athletic participation, especially in basketball, and at a time when Title IX had perhaps gained more energy than ever, girls and women were being recognized big-time for their physical strengths and abilities.

When I first looked back on this time, I thought that girls would have embraced and celebrated each other's achievements, regardless of how they participated in the sport. Yet, it seemed that the changed image of women's athletics had actually increased the acceptability of covert and overt aggression among females during basketball games.

AAU girls trash-talked to each other even more than the little league boys did to me, but unlike boys, the girls' verbal attacks weren't geared so much toward skill as they were appearance. And unlike my take on competition, these girls didn't consider boys their main opposition; they were each other's main opposition.

While not all girls that played AAU were disrespectful toward their teammates or opponents (I actually formed some of the most rewarding and memorable friendships of my life in AAU), those who were disrespectful weren't hesitant to express their emotions. Before games, when my team walked into a gym in front of our opponents, some of them would sharply say, "Here come the Barbies," or they would sarcastically call us "The Golden Girls" (many of us had sun-kissed skin and sun-streaked hair). Mean glares and chuckles always followed such remarks.

While playing the game, these slams usually escalated into physical retaliations aimed against our bodily features. If we would put defensive pressure on these opponents, they would say something like, "Get off me bitch," and then shove us in the chest while making a cut to the ball. They would also pull our hair when the referees weren't looking, and if we fell down, one of them might stand on our ponytail until we screamed, or swung at their legs, or an official intervened. If the outcome of the game didn't result in our opponents' favor, they would at least leave us with a bruised body and confidence. Then, after the game, our opponents would recruit their parents to fight with our parents about whose daughter had said what and who had hurt whose feelings.

I hardly ever remember playing in a tournament where these types of incidents didn't take place in at least one game. Rather than coming together to forward the progress of female athletic participation, our team united in order to survive our own gender. While playing AAU de-emphasized my clash with boys, I still didn't consider girls my number one and only competition, even when I would get caught-up in physically and emotionally defending my teammates or myself. So, after my first few AAU seasons, I was always ready to return to an environment in which I could clinch "W's" and feel better about myself in the process.

When the summer season came to an end, I used church activities as an outlet to release my competitive emotions. Here, I was back in my element, able to vie against boys. Here, there existed a mutual understanding of open competitiveness. Here, the most sought-out position wasn't point guard, but acolyte. Sunday school was a race to see who could look up Bible verses fastest. Youth choir was a battle of who could belt-out songs the loudest, and at Christmas the challenge was to see who could jingle the largest bell in the bell ensemble. I loved the praise I received when I was recognized for these activities, and I thought that because I was commended, no one would ever think or say anything bad about me.

However, I grew discouraged from participating in church activities not when the boys gloated about defeating me but when I became alarmed by some of the members' lies and gossip. The wrongness of these actions weighed heavy upon me; it was something that I had learned about several years earlier, while rummaging through the drawer of our living room coffee table. In the drawer, I had found an illustrated book of the Ten Commandments. Whenever I would flip through its pages, I would always get stuck on the picture of the Ninth Commandment, which stated, "You shall not give false testimony against your neighbor" (Exodus 20:16). The illustration showed a Roman soldier holding an infant upside down. He pointed a sword at the baby, overlooking its pleading mother. In the background was a king on his throne, and off to the left was a woman ducking-out of the scene. With her back turned toward the chaos, she concealed her identity under a hooded cloak and looked at the infant out of the corners of her eyes, as if she was pleased that the other woman's baby was going to be killed.

In sorting through the drawer of odds and ends, I found a penny and used it to scratch-out the pupils of the sinister-looking woman. The entire illustration bothered me, but she angered me more than any character, because her expression suggested she had broken the Ninth Commandment. After reading the accompanying description of the commandment, which warned against lying, gossiping, and harshly criticizing, I was certain that some devious action the woman had taken or some lie she had told was the cause of the baby's unfortunate predicament. I was annoyed that this woman appeared to want the baby to die, but more so, I was hurt that she could turn against another woman in this way. Every time I skimmed through the book, I stopped on the same page, convinced there were other women in the world who were just as capable of acting in such a wicked way.[37]

I had seen the Ninth Commandment broken in my community, in AAU, and now I had seen it broken in church, where it seemed that people would be socially executed by rumors, whispers, and dirty looks if they weren't willing to go along with the viewpoints and decisions of the members that had authority.

I first noticed this scenario play out with my parents. When they declined director positions of the church board and daycare, which they had been appointed to without their consent, the members (husband and wife tandems) who had delegated the responsibilities began to glower at Mom and Dad from across the sanctuary.

I remember several times that my parents encountered these members in public. Mom or Dad would express a salutation or try to start a conversation, but the members would either be extremely curt or totally disregard my parents, and it wasn't long until these members' friends started acting in the same manner. I can only speculate this treatment arose because Mom and Dad had defied established authority, and their noncompliance posed a threat to the members' power.

I had seen people turn on Miss Sally, our youth choir director, too. One day after choir practice, I listened to several moms speak of how they had heard a head member say that Miss Sally had started closing the doors of practice because she was teaching witchcraft.

Because Miss Sally was a sweet, involved lady, I found the remarks preposterous and thought that all the adults would think so too. However, after the rumor spread, some of the participants and followers of the group actually bought into the idea that Miss Sally was a witch. I didn't know if Miss Sally had also defied the head members' authority, but for whatever reason, it was as if the rumor had been spread with the intent to sabotage her reputation. Sadly, the efforts to isolate Miss Sally worked. Shortly after this incident, her attendance lessened, and she eventually left the church permanently.

As time went on, I saw similar incidents happen to several other individuals and families. It seemed as if many of these occurrences usually began with women, but when direct action was needed, the women seemed to cower behind their spouses. Rarely did the women continue to deal with the conflict that they initiated. Instead, they handed over their issue to their husbands and left them to end the problem.

Noticing that this peer aggression took place among both women and men left me wondering if I would have to put up with such actions for the rest of my life. I expected this behavior from preadolescent AAU girls but not from church-attending, Christian adults, the very people who were called to abide by the Golden Rule. Although lying and gossiping were supposed to be unacceptable, I never saw any actions taken to correct it, even after it created conflicts, ruined friendships, and alienated those who were victimized. Rather, it was always viewed as a standard part of life that simply happened and had to be tolerated. Because of this expectation, I began to consider that church was a dispiriting place. I cared less whether or not I attended, and soon I wouldn't have to attend.[38]

Once my next AAU season began, my family took the opportunity to travel to tournaments all over the eastern United States. Our absorption in basketball led to more than just weekend gym hopping expeditions, though. It sent us on a nine-year departure from church. Instead of spending Sundays singing hymns and listening to an hour sermon, our holy ritual became collecting titles, trophies, ribbons, and medals.

It might seem as if my absence from church caused me to place more value in basketball than in faith, but I never abandoned Christianity when my family left church. I continued to trust that God loved me, and Jesus died for me; those things I never questioned, that is, until my senior year of high school.

Throughout high school, basketball remained my central focus. In addition, I also became occupied with numerous other extracurricular activities that had my name echoing through the loudspeakers and parading the pages of local newspapers. Regularly doused with compliments and support from friends, acquaintances, and strangers, my inner confidence soared. It was then that I loved my community. I felt a great sense of pride in knowing that if I represented my community well, it would represent me well in return. It was simple. If I always acted as a proper, polite young lady, I would be accepted. Abiding by this plan made me feel so safe and satisfied that I forgot about my goal to prevent slanderous gossip. However, this lax attitude kept me distracted from the reality that I could not prevent relational aggression from lurking in the shadows of praise.

The Power of a Powder-puff

It was several years earlier, in middle school, that I recall my first major bouts with relational aggression. In fifth grade, students from my district's elementary schools merged into one school, doubling our class size, thus doubling my sports competition.

On my first day of fifth grade, I ran on to the playground with eager eyes, looking for the sorry boy who would be my first victim. Scanning the area, I noticed that the new guys looked bigger. I paused for a few minutes to plan how I would maintain my tough-girl status. It was time to walk a little taller, dribble a little faster, and talk the talk of the big boys.

During my first few recesses, I got into some pretty rough pickup games. All of a sudden, it was much more difficult to hang with the guys. Still, I was willful. Disregarding my stinging, skinned knees and elbows, I would limp out of the nurse's office decorated in Band-Aids, ready to begin placing bets again. I wasn't the only ambitious girl in my class, though. Several other girls shared similar aspirations. One was every bit as competitive as me, but defeating boys wasn't what interested her.

Her name was Sara, and she was the most popular girl from the other side of the district. On the playground, she was a quick sprinter and a strong-kickin' soccer striker. Although we shared an interest in athletics, I was more attracted to her older-girl image. Sara was experienced in areas in which I was clueless. She brought forth a world of padded underwire bras, Nair, cuticle cutters, Covergirl compacts, and Guess jeans. The need for these things baffled me, and my introduction to them implied that there was something icky about my hairy legs, chewed nails, sweat-beaded face, and barely A-cup chest. Still, I gravitated toward Sara's advanced knowledge, and shortly after we met, we declared sisterhood—short-termed sisterhood, that is.

Not long after we united, I realized that my friendship with Sara wasn't as attractive as I had once thought. Sara was one of the first girls in our class to emphasize the importance of maintaining a flawless, eye-catching appearance. She would constantly comment on how pretty she was, and she was always gazing into mirrors and windows, or proclaiming that her bust had grown. Plus, whenever she bought a new outfit she might as well have held a playground price check. Because I had learned that appearance and material items were not to be boasted about, I began to get aggravated by Sara's announcements.

Sara's obsession with appearance wasn't the only thing that irritated me. When we played games, she would always change the rules so she would win. Nearly every time I informed her of my crushes, Sara began dating them within a week. Then she would boast to me about the bases that she had reached with them. Another turn-off was that she constantly made mean remarks about people when they weren't around; then acted nicely in their presence. She also wrote lists of the most popular and least popular students to determine who could and couldn't be our friends. Despite her dominant, abrasive behavior, my classmates and I were entranced by what we viewed as her "maturity." She would crack her jump rope, and we would do anything she demanded.

I remember feeling pressured to help Sara pick the coolest friends on the playground. To determine this, we would hide behind a huge Oak tree at the edge of the schoolyard, and whenever anyone interrupted our meeting, Sara would shout, "No! Go away. You can't be back here," and I would follow her lead in being exclusive. Being Sara's sidekick made me feel empowered, as if I had been specifically selected to do important jobs for her.

However, after I saw that our exclusiveness made others feel rejected, I started to wonder why I was her friend. I didn't like hurting peoples' feelings. Plus, *never* had I wanted bases to refer to French kissing and going "up the shirt," and if I spent more than a couple of minutes looking at myself in the mirror, it was only to see if I had successfully stained a red Kool-Aid mustache to my upper lip.

Sara was that friend who told me Kool-Aid mustaches weren't cool. Now, I see that Sara was my first friend who indirectly advised me to measure my self-worth based on how others, particularly boys, perceived me.[39] She had been like no other friend I had ever had. Sara had taken competition beyond playground games, and the more I noticed our conflicting ideas of competition and the more I got pulled into arguments, the more I became annoyed, and the less I wanted to be her friend.[40]

Sara's competitiveness wasn't an oh-so-you-think-you're-better-than-me-well-let's-go-out-to-the-field-and-find-out type of thing. It was more of an unspoken challenge meant to stay hidden from everyone. While it was fine for her to show her need to win on the baseball diamond or in a 100-yard dash, it wouldn't be acceptable if she openly acted and competed in the same way outside of sports. Announcing that she was going to rival or control me or any other girl would have caused her to be frowned upon by adults and rejected by classmates.[41]

In middle school, I didn't understand Sara's ringleader mentality, but I did observe that she was willing to compete in ways that I wasn't. I needed out. It had been perfect timing when she falsely blamed me for calling a girl a bitch. That was when, on the playground, in front of all of our friends, I reclaimed my independence by defiantly telling Sara that I didn't want to be her friend and that she wasn't going to boss me around any longer.

To me, our divergence wasn't a big deal. Up until I was a young adult, I had always felt as if it had been a typical part of youth, one of the many times where I changed friends in order to find who I meshed best with. Little had I known then that I would be made to pay for my decision for years to come. In hindsight, I can see how my unladylike, face-to-face rejection of Sara had created a harsh embarrassment to her. It made things personal, because surely, if I wasn't with her, I was against her. My actions didn't conform adequately to the definition of femininity—the very definition that Sara was striving to meet—and for this, I would be punished for the rest of my life.[42]

While I reverted to touch football and dodgeball, Sara began spitting her resentment of me into everyone else's lunch milk. Throughout middle school and junior high, she would say to her friends, "See how Tami's sitting at *that* lunch table? She won't be my friend 'cause she *hates* me."

Soon enough, everyone knew that I allegedly despised Sara. One boy even told me that she had told him that I was jealous of her. I insisted that I wasn't, but he had been convinced otherwise. Every time I pointed out Sara's behavior to her or to others, she would flip things around and blame me for doing exactly what she had done to me. Back then I didn't understand why people believed the things that she said about me. However, now I see how she was able to set up this perception.

Sara was the first girl in our fifth grade class to claim popularity when she announced that she wanted to become homecoming queen her senior year of high school. I had first heard of this before our breakup, while we were still friends. Sara had come to my house for a sleep over, and while sitting at our kitchen island bar, she informed Mom and me of her goal. Mom sarcastically told her, "What a goal," but I never said anything. After I saw Mom's reaction, I just sat there with a what-the-heck-was-that-all-about expression. Something about this discussion was off. I didn't know what a homecoming queen was, but after I found out, I thought Sara's goal to be a little premature and off-track. To me, high school felt as if it were a bazillion years away. At eleven years old, I was only focused on the next few days, but there was much more planning going on in Sara's mind, and when I returned to school the following week, I found out that her desire to win homecoming queen was something she had also informed many of the other girls about.

While there was nothing wrong with Sara wanting to be popular and wanting to earn a reward, the weaponry she used in attempting to secure the title was problematic.

From fifth grade on, Sara's reign held strong. Few classmates ever challenged her position or questioned her authority because they didn't want to put themselves in the same position as I had, as a target of her meanness.[43]

After I had broken-off our friendship and denied Sara the ability to control me, I created a power shift, a threat to her goal. Needing some way to express her aggression toward me, she developed a strategy that would showcase my flaws, help her regain command, and safeguard her own self-interest.[44]

Sara lived by the cliché, "keep your friends close and your enemies closer." She kept me close alright. She constantly held my attention by forcing me to focus on the unrelenting aggravation that she could and would cause.

Through our previous friendship, Sara had become acquainted with my weaknesses. She had seen my temper surface when people had called me profane names and told lies about me, and she made sure to target me where I was weakest.[45]

Her first step was to spread rumors that would force me to initiate confrontation. Then, when I approached her, asking why she had lied about me, she would say that she didn't. Unconvinced, I would blow-up and leave angry. After I exited, Sara would secure her innocence by shrugging her shoulders to her surrounding peers, saying that she had no idea why I was so irate. Sara did all of this to get under my skin without having anyone detect her doings.[46]

As this scenario became repetitious, many of our classmates began to view our disputes as a result of my inability to control my anger and competition.[47] Plus, because I never stuck around to work things out and make amends, it showed that I really must have hated her. Although I didn't want to be friends with Sara, and I did call her "bitch" whenever she made me angry, I didn't display frustration toward her because I loathed her. I just wanted her to leave me alone and to stop saying fictitious things about me. Yet, for the remainder of our schooling, Sara's schemes caused our classmates to hold preconceived notions about my acquaintanceship with her.[48]

Sara wasn't going to do all the work alone, though. She needed to turn as many people as she could against me, so it would prevent them from turning against her.[49]

Throughout junior high, I lost about four friends to Sara. No matter how much I telephoned my lost comrades or asked them to spend the night or to go to the movies, they simply wanted nothing to do with me any longer. I would say "hi" to them at lunch and in the hallways or class, but they would roll their eyes or ignore me. Their spontaneous decision to stop associating with me left me perplexed and offended. According to studies conducted by Joyce Benenson and Deborah Bennaroch, it was possible that my former friends might have felt that I was in some way superior to them or more successful than them, and, as a result, I would eventually abandon them, just as I had abandoned Sara.[50]

Whatever the reasons, my former friends related to Sara's enmity for me. It was a connection that destabilized my foundation of support, increased Sara's power, and gave my ex-friends a stronger sense of social belonging.[51] It also assured that Sara would never have to take sole blame for her aggression toward me. Through this bond, Sara furtively assumed the role of Queen Bee, and her newfound friends became her "Honeybees."[52] Author Rachel Simmons best describes this process of alliance building in the following:

> Nothing launches a girl faster, or takes her down harder, than alliance building, or "ganging up." The ultimate relational aggression, alliance building forces the victim to face not only the potential loss of the relationship with her opponent, but with many of her friends. It goes like this: Spotting a conflict on the horizon, a girl will begin a scrupulous underground campaign to best her opponent. Like a skilled politician, she will methodically build a coalition of other girls willing to throw their support behind her. Friends who have "endorsed" her will ignore the target, lobby others for support, or confront the target directly until she is partly or completely isolated.[53]

On the contrary, the Honeybees did a better job at isolating themselves. They developed a mean-girl status that made them popularly unpopular.[54] However, these girls weren't replicas of those prissy princesses in teen flicks like *Mean Girls, She's All That, Never Been Kissed, Jawbreaker,* or *Heathers.* They didn't strut down the halls in synchronous, slow-mo stride with their hair blowing in a breeze, slathered in lip-gloss and eye shadow. Nor did they accessorize pleated, plaid miniskirts and popped-collar crop tops with Prada bags or Gucci sunglasses. People didn't run into opened locker doors or trip into garbage cans when they saw them. In fact, I had heard a lot of schoolmates make fun of them when they weren't around, and many classmates said they didn't like them because they were domineering, just like the characters in those popular mean-girl movies.

I was glad people were finally starting to see the Honeybees the same way that I did, but I couldn't seem to get anyone to take a stand against them with me. There was just something about a face-to-face encounter with a Honeybee that made mouths zip. It was as if everyone was afraid of being punished. No one wanted to make the Honeybees angry because the girls would find a way to embarrass them or get them in trouble with a teacher, a parent, or an older sibling, and as eighth grade approached, the girls gained plenty of practice at this. It was then that the Honeybees became more like Wasps—increasingly aggressive and more powerful with each sting.

In a junior high school newspaper poll, it seemed as if the Honeybee's meanness scared our classmates into voting for Sara as the most popular girl in our grade, but many of our peers became turned off by her boasting about the title. Finally, I wasn't the only one who was sick of her bragging, and it was at this time that Sara's popularity climaxed.

In the fall of our freshman year of high school, Sara campaigned for homecoming attendant, confident that she would be chosen. However, in eighth grade, I had made many new friends, and our classmates elected me instead. It was in building relationships with the "less than A-list" and simply treating other students how I wanted to be treated that I proved popular kids didn't have to be mean and exclusive. However, the satisfaction I received from this award was short-lived, as Sara made sure to counter my merit. With my popularity increasing and her popularity decreasing, she embarked on a serious mission to regain her reign.[55]

By the end of the day, Sara began telling everyone that I had spread rumors about her sexual escapades. I had no idea what she was talking about. Like always, I felt inclined to defend myself and dispute the accusations. When I confronted her, alone in the hallway instead of in front of a group at lunch, she insisted that I had spread the rumors. Frustrated, I told her that I hadn't, and to get a life and move on from picking on me.

Several class periods later, her upperclassman boyfriend, Kent, approached me. While I was walking down the stairs, he stood above, yelling that I needed to leave the two of them alone. Then he launched his chewed gob of gum at my head. Luckily, he missed. After this, Sara, with Kent, definitely took my advice to move on, as they proceeded, with their parents, to picking on my parents.

Mom and one of her best friends, JoAnn, were the next to endure Sara and Kent's tactics. While Mom and Jo were at the county fair, an oncoming truck forced them off a walkway. The driver drove so close that Mom and Jo were nearly run-over. He forced them to jump down into a ditch filled with large, broken pieces of concrete that had been left over from recent construction. It took them a quick second to realize that they weren't hurt. Then they yelled at the driver to watch where he or she was going. That was when they noticed Kent at the steering wheel and Sara by his side. Mom and Jo were infuriated but unable to confront Sara and Kent because they had driven away.

That night, a sheriff deputy left a message on our answering machine. He said that Sara's parents had filed a complaint against Mom for harassing Sara and that Sara's parents wanted Mom to leave their daughter alone.

After retrieving the message, my parents paced around for about 20 minutes, red in the face. Then Dad called Sara and Kent's parents and returned the threat to take legal action if either tried to uphold the charges.

A short time after this occurrence, a new family moved into one of our neighboring houses. The significance of this was that a relative of the family, Mr. Smith, worked in law enforcement, and it wasn't long before my parents became acquainted with him through basketball.

In a conversation with him, Mom and Dad mentioned the message that was left on our answering machine. The ordeal sounded odd to Mr. Smith. He said that if a complaint had been filed, the deputy should have arrived at our home with documentation. He promised to check into it. Several days passed, and Mr. Smith confirmed the deputy never filed the complaint. With my parents, Mr. Smith came up with the notion that Sara's family must have used their acquaintanceship with the deputy to cause us the hassle.

Looking back, I understand why Sara's parents behaved in this way. Not only had I embarrassed and rejected their daughter when I ended our friendship, now I had been voted as the first homecoming attendant in our class, a position which was supposed to be awarded to Sara. Naturally, Sara's parents wanted happiness and success for their daughter. However, I was becoming Sara's most annoying roadblock, and this caused her parents to adopt and express some of the same ill feelings Sara experienced. Trying to intimidate my parents by threatening to press charges against my mom was a way for Sara's parents to get back at me through creating a more acceptable and level playing ground.

During the time that followed the fair incident, Sara didn't create many conflicts. As a freshman and sophomore, she won several academic and extracurricular awards. Sara and I didn't compete in the same sports or clubs, so I didn't feel defeated by her accomplishments. I was actually glad she won, and I thought that her achievements would provide her with enough satisfaction and confidence to quit badmouthing me. Conversely, the recognition only intensified her competitiveness toward me.[56] It was as if Ethel Merman's song "Anything You Can Do" was programmed to play in Sara's mind every time she saw me succeed at something.

During the spring of my junior year, not long after I had set a school basketball record, participated on the most successful girls' basketball team in our school's history, and recorded an anti-alcohol and drug radio commercial for a local station, Sara and her Honeybees started harassing me more than ever. For these accomplishments, my classmates, teachers, and community commended me on being an example of leadership and responsibility. The Honeybees, however, didn't share the same opinions. They waited until several weeks later, at the prom, to communicate their feelings about my image.

That year, I had been on the prom decorating committee. I had been honored to be part of such decision-making. I had been the only girl among three boys, so my feminine opinion had been asked for often. After the junior and senior classes had voted for the theme, the four of us agreed on city-themed decorations and placed an order. Of course, the Honeybees weren't pleased with our choices, mainly because I played a significant role in the decision-making.

I learned that the Honeybees had been telling everyone that I wasn't on the committee, that *they* were the committee. They had even obtained several of the committee's decoration books and tried to muster enough support to change the décor.

Seeing as prom is an important event to most high school students, this was causing quite a stir, because everyone thought the details had already been determined. While this was one situation that the Honeybees didn't alter, this would be the last time they would tolerate any decision that I helped make.

Prior to prom, I worried whether the decorations would stay in place. My anxiety subsided as I spent hours excitedly preparing for the big celebration. On the day of the dance, I created a curly up-do, applied more eyeliner and blush than usual, and doused my neck and wrists with Calvin Klein's Escape. After I slipped on my baby pink dress and glittery, pink four-inch heels (definitely not the appearance that I would have agreed on several years earlier), my date arrived (an hour late). Mom snapped a couple of photos, and then with several other couples we headed off to a charming inn for dinner.

When we arrived at prom, I was pleased to see that the balloons were still floating, and the streamers were still strung from the ceiling. Many students told our committee that the decorations were fabulous, much better than the previous year's. As I stood in line for photographs, I was tempted to locate the Honeybees and tell them "I told you so," but I kept it to myself.

With my confidence and pride on the rise, I swayed my shoulders and hips to the comeback of Vanilla Ice's "Ice Ice Baby." With about 15 friends, I found my way to the center of the empty dance floor, and we began showcasing a bizarre mix of disco-hoedown moves. Despite our lack of elegance, we were entertained. The evening was turning into one of those warm, scrapbook memories, but that changed when one of my friends told me to turn around.

That's when I saw *them*. Amber, Chelsea, and Dawn, three of Sara's Honey-bees, were about ten feet behind me, and Sara and Kent stood behind them, against a wall. They were all laughing, pointing at, and mocking my dance moves. They had sent me a message through one of my male friends: "She looks like shit. Her hair's dumb, and her dress is ugly." Over the loud music, I yelled for them to stop and to get a life. I returned a cold stare then gave them the finger and fell in rhythm with the Chicken Dance.

I was able to ignore them for a while, but after prom I couldn't escape Amber. As I was exiting the building, she walked up to me and scornfully said, "We weren't talking about you." Then, in passing, she ran her shoulder into mine, knocking me backward.[57]

"What's your problem!?" I asked, but Amber kept walking as if she didn't hear me. My friends and Amber's date stared, speechless. I could tell they were waiting for me to retaliate, but instead I turned to a few friends to discuss what Amber's "deal" was. Then, without further confrontation, I left with my friends.

I was familiar with the Honeybees' disgust for me, but this had been the bold-est attack yet. When their harassment had first begun, they only gave me dirty looks, called me names like "bitch," "slut," "stuck-up," "goodie-goodie," and "rich snob," and told people that I said bad things about them. Then they moved to putting down my character and picking apart any little thing about me. They dissed everything from why I was always smiling to how I ran and what clothes I wore, and they frequently made fun of my long, thick, blonde hair. They called it "the horse's tail" or commented on how ratty they thought it was. When Sara and I were friends, she even tried to equalize us by telling me that my hair would look a lot better if I cut it short like her hair. She would fold my hair under the nape of my neck or tuck it under a hat and say, "See how much better it would look?" Sometimes, when I was dressed nicely for school, the girls would tell peo-ple that I looked like a 12-year-old or if I didn't wear makeup they told me I looked tired or asked if I was sick. Every time my picture made the front page of the sports section, they mocked my facial expression. They even bashed my faith. One time, in response to a quote I had made in the newspaper in which I had said that I would give anything to meet God, they laughed and said it was the stupidest thing they had ever heard because no one knew if there really was a God.[58]

Everything that made me feel good about myself, that I considered to be my strengths, was what the Honeybees punished me for. The girls loved poking fun at me; most likely because tearing me down bonded them closer. According to Dr. Mary Pipher, author of *Reviving Ophelia: Saving the Selves of Adolescent Girls*, it is common for girls to "punish by picking a certain girl, usually one who is relatively happy, and making her life miserable." It was as if the Honeybees made remarks and gestures that made me doubt myself and feel less attractive, that way they would feel more confident and more appealing.[59]

Now, I recognize that the reasons for Sara's behaviors were more than just a toxic rivalry with me. Years after high school, I learned the women in Sara's family had treated other girls and woman similarly to how Sara had treated me. It was as if the females in Sara's family had casually imbedded and passed down relationally aggressive behavior.

While in high school, Sara's aunt Regina had bullied Faith, one of my family acquaintances. Once, when Faith was talking to Rob, one of her male friends, Regina, with one of her friends, went to a payphone and called Rob's girlfriend, Becca, to tell her Faith was flirting with Rob. Rob walked in on the girls' phone call, but he arrived too late to repair the damage that had been done to Faith. Rob warned Faith that Becca was angry and that she would be coming to that week's football game, where both Faith and Regina would be cheerleading.

At the game, Becca sat in the bleachers and glared at Faith. This visibly bothered Faith, and when Regina saw this, she told Faith, "Don't be angry at *me*. *I* didn't do anything." Faith restrained herself as best as possible, telling Regina, "Leave me the hell alone," and, "Get away from me before I say something I shouldn't say." When Regina's mother (Sara's grandmother) saw and learned about this conflict, she immediately took the matter to the principal. During the game, the principal pulled Faith and Regina aside and asked Faith if she had said "hell." Faith confessed and, in turn, the principal suspended her from the cheerleading squad.

Regina and her friends also spread rumors about Faith's "promiscuity." Faith had a lot of male friends, and Regina was always trying to steal Faith's boyfriend or get her boyfriend to break up with her. Regina and her friends would constantly accuse Faith of "sleeping around" and cheating, and they even recruited enough classmates to vote Faith as "Class Flirt," hoping Faith's boyfriend would get angry at this and break up with her.

Regina even told a teacher that she saw Faith cheating on a test, and because the teacher believed Regina, he made sure Faith wasn't inducted into the National Honor Society, even though Faith's grade point average qualified her for initiation.

Now, through Faith's experiences, I see that Sara's aggression had less to do with solely attacking me and more to do with how she learned to compete against other girls. However, back when I was in school, I felt as if there were no reasons for Sara and her friends' attacks. At first, I returned their mean glares and words because it seemed to be the only way to protect my self-worth. After these "eye for an eye" episodes, I always questioned the Honeybees' behaviors, and my family and friends told me that the girls were just jealous, like it was supposed to be a compliment and an honor to have girls feel less valuable in comparison to me. I was told that I shouldn't "stoop to their level," and that I should ignore them because enduring their hostility would strengthen my character. So, instead of fighting with the Honeybees, I dismissed their innuendoes and actions as petty teenage drama and pretended as though their behavior didn't bother me—except their behavior *did* bother me. Asserting moral authority and ignoring their harassment didn't prevent my being bullied—the strategies would *never* protect me from the Honeybees' aggression. Every time I acted as though I wasn't hurt or offended, the girls thought their plan had backfired. Thus, their rivalry against me heightened, and they wouldn't stop until they conquered me.[60]

Delegating Dirty Work

As the Honeybees' plan to overthrow me continued to develop, Sara slipped into the background and Amber, Chelsea, and Dawn stepped up to play-out the group's aggression. I now see that they were a versatile trio, each able to play many roles such as Sidekick, Banker, Floater, and Pleaser/Wannabe/Messenger.[61] Most likely, the three rallied around Sara not only to be affiliated with social desirability but also because they eliminated themselves from being targeted, and because they treasured the authority and unity that came with treating me badly.[62] I had a history with all of them.

Sara's wannabe was Amber. She had moved into our school district in junior high. She didn't play sports and wasn't involved in many clubs, but that hadn't prevented Sara from quickly recruiting her as she had tried to do with every new female student. Within weeks of Amber's enrollment, our personalities clashed. She constantly gossiped about me to me in front of our entire math class. She would make bogus comments like, "I heard you don't like so-and-so," or "So-and-so said you called her friend a bitch." We had several I-can't-stand-you spats, though I don't recall what triggered them or what they were about. Nonetheless, our conflicts were enough to send Amber bee lining to the other side.

Dawn was Sara's primary banker. Dawn and I had called ourselves best friends in elementary and middle school. Nearly every weekend, we would sleep over at each other's house. Well, actually we didn't do much sleeping. We usually stayed up until daybreak, and our parents had to get up several times throughout the night to hush our giggling. It had been cool hanging out with Dawn because she was so involved in our school. She was always attending some type of athletic event, because her brother was an athlete, and her parents helped out with a lot of school programs. I loved when she asked me to go with her. Being the oldest child in my family, it was rare that I experienced the atmosphere of high school sports without Dawn's invitation. It was when we finally made it to high school that, without warning, Dawn terminated our friendship. I was hurt and baffled by her decision, and as time passed, I saw no other choice but to replace Dawn with a new friend.

However, I had the most bad blood with Chelsea, who was also a banker, a messenger, and a contender to become Sara's sidekick. In middle school and junior high, we had been on and off again friends, mainly because we were gymnastics teammates. She had told people that I was a slut, and she had frequently given me dirty looks. She had also given me problems when she tried to steal my boyfriend.

After Chelsea started calling me names, Mom asked a guidance counselor to mediate. Chelsea and I met with the counselor, but she denied saying anything about me. After the meeting, the counselor recommended that my parents contact Chelsea's parents to discuss the incidents that had occurred between us. Dad placed a call to Kim, Chelsea's mom, but he realized he had failed to get through when all Kim responded with was, "Yeah, so what's your point?" Kim's reaction disappointed me. I felt that she condoned Chelsea's behavior, and because of this, the issues between Chelsea and I would never be resolved.

In high school, the amount of time Chelsea and I spent together on the gymnastics team virtually disappeared as I played varsity, and Chelsea mostly played junior varsity. During a competition in which our school's bitter rival was outmatching us, I finished my floor routine, and after sitting down and leaning back on our bench, I took a few chugs from a water bottle then carelessly tossed it behind me. It hit the bleacher and squirted an opposing fan, who was standing nearby. He yelled at me. I apologized and said that I didn't mean to get him wet, but Chelsea and another teammate, neither of whom had seen me toss the water bottle (they were standing with their backs toward me, watching the activity at the opposite end of the gym), scolded me for "deliberately" dousing him. I was insulted that they defended a rival fan over me, their own teammate, however, at the same time, I was not surprised. This wouldn't be the last problem Chelsea caused.

Once in the locker room, everyone had been talking about Gina, an ex-Honeybee who wasn't well-liked among the student body. "Did you hear her boyfriend got arrested for shoplifting a pregnancy test?" Chelsea asked. The room erupted with scoffs, and I made the mistake of joining in the laughter and prodding. I didn't like Gina, and I felt safe knowing that it was the same opinion that the other girls were sharing, but I had overlooked Chelsea's presence.

Within an hour or so, people were coming up to me saying Gina wanted to fight me. I met her in the hallway where I learned that Chelsea had told Gina that I was leading the locker room gossip because I hated Gina and wanted her go to jail with her boyfriend. A crowd surrounded and urged us to fight, but when I looked around and saw that Chelsea was no where to be found, I simply walked away, realizing it was Chelsea's goal to create a conflict that would get me in trouble.

After this, I made sure to keep my mouth shut, especially around Chelsea. Thankfully, as a senior, finally I didn't have to worry about her locker room instigations because she chose not to compete. However, socially, Chelsea was still in the game.

After informing my parents of what had happened with the Honeybees at prom, Dad contacted one of my school's trusted administrators, Mr. Littlefield. Although he never disciplined Amber for shoulder-shoving me after prom, he seemed to be concerned. He advised us to start documenting harassments. He also said that he wanted to know about any problems that I experienced, even if they occurred off school property.

Naturally, I became even more defensive when dealing with the Honeybees. As a child, one thing I had learned from competing on the basketball court and on the playground was to stand up for myself. I had never let boys get away with taunting my athletic ability, and I wasn't about to let the Honeybees make fun of my physical appearance or personality. Everyone already thought that I hated Sara and her friends, so I wasn't afraid to display my anger toward them because I didn't think I had anything to lose if I opposed them. I started to realize this several years earlier, when I was in junior high.

However, in eighth grade and in early ninth grade, I also learned that in order to be admired by others, I was required to make some adjustments. While at lunch and in study hall, as my friends and I skimmed the pages of *Seventeen* and *YM*, I saw that if I were to maintain my status, I needed to surrender my tomboy image to the role society intended for me. It was the same type of revelation Sara had had years earlier.

I saw that it wasn't a young girl's purpose to be a hard-hitter or tough-talker. Neither was it acceptable to retaliate in any situation.[63] The key was not to act too boy-like, something I had been doing for a while. Now, as I was restricted by society from joining in on the guys' games, I sat in the stands as a spectator and studied the distinctions between our genders. While I had been caught-up in outperforming boys, my magazines and T.V. shows were urging me to shine for boys and outshine girls in the process. So, to please everyone, I put all of my effort into playing the "perfect" girl game.

I tucked away my stand-up-and-fight voice, turned my anger toward the Honeybees inward, watered down my ambition, and became constrained by my gender role.[64] Instead, I lit-up a charming, flirty smile and became a social sweetheart. I switched out my oversized sweaters and loose fitting Levi's with form fitting tee shirts, low-rise flares, and short skirts. I uncomfortably slept in foam curlers, filled my bathroom cabinet with Cover Girl and Maybelline, and sweated it out in the tanning bed. I even bought a Wonderbra. Transformed, I became what seemed to be an illustration of society's ideal, late-twentieth-century girl, as I gracefully mixed the slightest bit of muscle and sweat with strappy heels and pink ribbons. My sexual makeover was made not only to win the boys' attention but to outdo my female competitors, specifically Sara. The game was officially on like it had never been before.[65]

It was in high school that I noticed the modifications proved successful, as I was elected to represent my school as a queen candidate in a local festival's beauty pageant. I had only beat out about seven other applicants, one of whom was Sara. Needless to say, she wasn't happy. Out of all the entrants, I had submitted the longest list of qualifications to the judges, but the facts didn't matter to Sara. She said that I didn't deserve the title. It was impossible for me to earn any achievement without stepping on Sara's toes. But at this point, I no longer cared how bruised and beaten she felt. I found pleasure in defeating her. I loved coming out on top over Sara because it seemed as if her sole purpose revolved around matching or exceeding my abilities and achievements. After all of the times that Sara had made me angry, I felt no guilt in returning the favor to her.

Sara didn't necessarily walk away empty handed, though. She could still participate in the festival by riding in the parade with her field hockey team. The issue with this was that while my car followed the field hockey team's float, Sara had to watch me smile, wave, and receive public admiration the entire procession. I had been in a similar "that should be me" position before. It was never pleasant when I had to watch an opposing basketball team make-off with the trophy that my team had worked so hard to attain, so I recognized how Sara must have felt toward me. Nonetheless, I still didn't care how my win made Sara feel.

The evening after the parade, I was to participate in the question-and-answer segment of the contest. This wasn't a tremendous deal to many people in our community. The only people that showed up to support me were my family and a few close friends ... and Amber and Dawn. I never understood why the two girls made the forty-five minute trip. They didn't admire me enough to support me. They must have come hoping to see me fail, and fail I did. I didn't win the pageant. I didn't even come in first, second, or third, but after the contest I did qualify as a target of more Honeybee hostility. What better way to defeat another girl than to shove her to make sure she stays down?

Whenever Amber saw me, whether in school or out of school, she would run her shoulder into mine without making verbal or eye contact.[66] She was about five or six inches taller and weighed at least 20 pounds more, features that she used to her advantage. Sometimes I would see her approaching out of my peripheral vision, so I could adjust my stance to where she would only knock me off balance. Other times, she would hit me from behind when I couldn't see her coming. It was then that I would fall into the lockers.

As these run-ins continued to take place, my ability to keep calm and to resist reacting lessened. My parents advised me to contain my feistiness. They said I should be the bigger person and walk away. They told me that Amber was trying to make me angry, because she knew she could easily provoke my temper.

Despite my frustration, I never retaliated, because I knew good girls weren't fighters. However, my parents and I knew that I would only be pushed so far. This wasn't like basketball. There was no referee to blow a whistle, and I feared the buzzer would never sound.

Amber's attacks didn't recede. After she plowed into me again while I was with two friends in a local store, my parents finally called a timeout. They contacted the sheriff's office, filed a complaint, and threatened to press charges, but before taking further action, they tried bringing the matter to the attention of Amber's parents. Unfortunately, my parents were never able to locate Amber's parents. Mom and Dad were informed by law enforcement that much of the time Amber had no consistent parental supervision. Her parents were divorced. Her dad wasn't around much, and her mom lived hundreds of miles away. As a result, Amber was often left in the care of her grandparents.

From what had been gathered, Amber was a stereotypical bully. It did not seem as if she had been living with a loving, nurturing, close-knit family. Therefore, she must have had a neglected childhood and bad home life. Whatever Amber experienced, Mom and Dad feared that pressing charges would make the situation worse; angering Amber enough to severely hurt me, maybe even kill me.

Amber's home life might have very well played a role in the physical abuse that she inflicted on me, but another explanation for her behavior was that Amber was dissatisfied with her lack of social power. For the most part, Amber was a Pleaser/Wannabe/Messenger. In order to gain more authority within the Honeybee alliance, she had to do something that the rest of the girls would not. Bullying me with physical aggression was the ultimate degradation. It solidified her loyalty to Sara, promoted her to Sidekick, and awarded her a higher sense of self-esteem.[67]

Unsupported Support

For the remainder of my junior year, Amber continued to knock into me as if I were invisible. Every time, I would tell my parents, who would then inform Mr. Littlefield. As an administrator, Mr. Littlefield was supposed to make sure that the anti-violence rule was implemented, but, every time, he asked only to be informed of any additional incidents, and whether they occurred in or out of school. I waited and waited for Mr. Littlefield to discipline Amber, trusting that he would provide me with protection. He had always cracked down on boys who had fought. Surely, the next time that Amber shoved me, he would see that she was suspended.

When it happened again, I went directly to the office. There, Ms. Pinkerton, the vice principal, seemed too preoccupied to consider the seriousness of my complaint. She told me that there was not much that could be done because I had no witnesses. The only thing I could do was fill-out an incident report, which she said she would give to the principal.

Weeks passed, and I was never questioned about the complaint. At that point, I was starting to get used to adult inattentiveness. This was not the first time that I had not been taken seriously.

I had been through this before, a few weeks after prom, when two of my friends found flyers about me at their homes. The flyers had my photograph scanned on them and labeled me my school's "nark." One flyer was posted on my friend's garage and the other was placed in my other friend's unlocked car. After learning the term was a slam against someone who rats out drug users to the police, I felt offended, because I assumed it was a slam against my clean record.

Curious as to whether anything could be found that would tell who had made the signs, my parents contacted the sheriff's detective bureau, and an investigator was sent to our house. He said that fingerprints would be too hard to pick-up off the papers, and that because we did not have any additional proof, we could not take action against anyone. He convinced us the signs were nothing to worry about, just teenage mischief that would soon blow over. Even my parents' attorney said that nothing could be done. Proof or no proof, the artists' identities were obvious to me. The girls behind these aggravations were becoming braver with the execution of every dirty deed.

Dad immediately communicated the incident to Mr. Littlefield, who was always willing to listen and assist—that is, if enough hard evidence was presented (and there was never enough hard evidence for his liking). On the surface, Mr. Littlefield seemed supportive and ready to encourage the school's mission statement and harassment policy, both of which vowed to provide students with secure, comfortable, and stimulating surroundings that were free from menace. However, as Amber initiated more physical contact, the rules continued to be neglected. She was never and would never be warned or disciplined for assaulting me.[68]

I did not understand why it was so difficult for Amber to be caught in action; there were only two short hallways in our small school. I assumed that Mr. Littlefield had alerted the staff about Amber's attacks against me, and I expected them to be on the lookout. Maybe they felt such precautions were unnecessary. Maybe to them this was just "girls being girls." Maybe they were part of the 25% of teachers that "see nothing wrong with bullying or putdowns and consequently intervene in only 4% of bullying incidents."[69] Maybe they thought that because nothing too dangerous had ever happened at our school, nothing extreme ever would.

Like most of my peers, I had always thought I could feel safe in my high school of only about 600. Characteristically, small schools offer a better sense of security. In them, virtually no student goes unaccounted for because adults are able to supervise better, and are more involved in students' lives and activities.[70] I believed I was protected in my school because it had always been a "we've got your back" type of atmosphere. But during a conversation with Mr. Littlefield, in which I expressed fear that Amber might try to inflict more harm against me, my faith in the safety of my school system was destroyed.

With the recent Columbine High School shootings (April 20, 1999), which had occurred just three weeks prior, I was uneasy. I felt compelled to bring my discomfort to Mr. Littlefield, especially because I attended a school where student farmers and hunters kept shotguns behind or under the seats in their unlocked pickup trucks. After all, the school shootings that started in the late '90s had happened at predominately white, small town or suburban facilities, and it was in small-town schools that 77% of adolescents reported being bullied.[71]

Telling Mr. Littlefield I was scared only made me feel like more of a crybaby idiot. He kept saying disciplinary action could not be enforced because I could not prove the girls were harassing me. As I persistently told him about my fears, he grew agitated, asking, "Has anyone threatened you with any type of weapon? No one has held a gun to your head have they?" When I said no, he told me that I had no reason to be scared. Sitting in front of his desk, I slid downward.

I was dumbfounded.

Speechless.

Disappointed.

Ashamed.

Why would Mr. Littlefield or any other administrator respond this way? There are several possible reasons. Like most adults, many school officials have not sought education about relational bullying or social development among adolescents. Therefore, they are unable to decipher serious, harmful problems from what might appear as "kids being kids." Due to this lack of understanding, a lot of administrators simply do not know how to handle these types of dilemmas and do not seek out preventative solutions. Likewise, some officials feel that bullying cannot be stopped because it is a moral issue and teaching ethics is not their responsibility, rather it is the responsibility of parents. Or, some administrators feel it is merely too late for them to make an impact on students' behaviors. Also, there are some school officials who feel that students should learn to independently handle their conflicts without adult guidance.[72]

Even if administrators are aware of relational bullying, they often do not take initiative to prevent it. In doing so, they would likely cause uproar within their community because the majority of society views passive aggression as tolerable and excusable. For that reason, it is easier for administrators to oppose social change within their school systems so that they meet public approval and avoid controversy, even if it means neglecting students' safety. Regardless of the reasons, rationales such as these signal a significant glitch in the efforts to improve educational and societal climates, as it has been found that one-third of students do not feel as if they are taken seriously when they bring their concerns about bullying to adults.[73]

Shortly after my meeting with Mr. Littlefield, I was so offended by his reaction that I was convinced he must have been plotting to ruin my life. *How could he not believe me!?* I thought. *Why didn't he take me seriously!?* He obviously did not have time to deal with my "paranoia." There was no way I could ever go back to him for help. His macho, not-in-my-school mentality not only contradicted the school's goal to safeguard students, it forced me to develop my own defensive coping mechanisms. Most of the time, I utilized my parents' recommendations to ignore derogatory remarks and to walk away when confronted, but my silence only intensified the conflict, causing the Honeybees to express even more resentment toward me by increasing the frequency of their name-calling and dirty looks.[74]

Unexpected Betrayal

I was relieved when my junior year of high school ended. I thought I would at least get a rest from the Honeybees' harassment. *Wrong*. No breaks on this break.

Early that summer I received an e-mail from an unfamiliar address, "noneyo-damnbidniz@fuckyou.com." Curious about its contents, I opened it. It was an e-greeting "Parents Day" card titled "a father's day poem that's MY dad." Its only message was "Watch yo' back."[75]

As I sat in front of our computer in the low lighting of our loft, I spent several minutes trying to figure out if I had actually been threatened or if I was just over-reacting. I sat motionless, except for my eyes. They rapidly scanned the screen, jumped to the wall behind the computer, back to the screen, to the surrounding desk area, and back again to the screen.

Arriving at the realization that I had been threatened, the message engulfed me. My breathing deepened, and I became lightheaded. I snapped out of what was soon to be hyperventilation when I heard my own muffled voice yell, "Mooom ... Daaad ... couja come here!?"

"Can ya wait a minute?" Mom shouted from outside.

"No. You need to come here, like now," I insisted.

Not yet informed of the situation, my parents made their way up the stairs relaxed. "Go ahead," I agitatedly said, shaking my finger at the computer. Their heads protracted toward the screen as if they were waiting for a translation. "W-h-a-t ... What the heck is *this*!?" they both asked, offended. This time this threat wouldn't be dismissed as just another high school prank.

Mom and Dad immediately contacted the sheriff's office and spoke with an investigator who provided them with instructions on how to trace the e-mail. First, they contacted the Web site from which the card had been sent. A representative of the site then gave them the sender's Internet Service Provider. Lastly, they contacted the provider who confirmed the sender's home address. Because Amber had physically attacked me, we were certain that she had sent the message. However, the Internet Service Provider revealed an unexpected location—the house of longtime family friends. I felt deceived and deeply offended.

One of the family's sons, Tyler, was my schoolmate and steadfast friend. As babies, we shared a playpen at our parents' get-togethers and cookouts, and as toddlers we attended each other's birthday parties. Upon entering kindergarten, our friendship was distanced as we attended different schools. After several years without seeing each other, we were able to revive our relationship in middle school, where we discovered our shared interest in basketball.

To present day, while rummaging through old boxes or envelopes, I happen upon pictures that display our mutual childhood affection. I even came across one that captured Tyler and I innocently smooching. Our young relationship seemed unwavering, but the e-mail exposed unexpected instability within our current friendship. I don't know why I never picked up on the possibility of Tyler turning against me, because over the years, Tyler had become a close friend of the Honeybees. In middle school, he had even dated Sara, and now, in high school, he was hooking up with Chelsea.

Tyler had always been known as a jokester, even though many students, including me, expressed annoyance with his comedic attempts. Everything he did, he tried to do humorously, and if his antics failed, he kept at them until someone chuckled. He was that kid who wrote the most random comments in everyone's yearbook. He was always the first to tell the new "Yo' mama" joke or to wear something "funny" like an afro-wig, oversized glasses, or rain boots when rain wasn't even in the forecast. At sporting events, he always heckled the opponents for everything from their athletic ability, to how much they perspired, to their sock length. Throughout the years, I had watched Tyler step up his act from drinking Elmer's glue to taste testing an array of Bath and Body Works lotions. He was always doing something of the sort.

The most memorable of his showcases took place during junior year. On several different occasions, I had watched him throw French fries at the learning disabled students who sat at the end of our lunch table. One day, he must have wasted a whole order pelting Winnie in the face. At first, she didn't appear pleased. Winnie seemed upset because she didn't understand why Tyler was being mean to her. But when Tyler laughingly asked, "It's fun, isn't it?" Winnie's cheeks lifted, and she began giggling until she burst into loud "ha ha ha's." As Winnie's large frame rocked back and forth, her deep, drawn-out, childlike voice sputtered, "Oh Tyler, yer so funny." His guy friends, unable to contain their snickering, looked away. I rolled my eyes to my nearby girlfriends and acted as though I didn't see what had happened.

Most of my classmates didn't make a big deal about Tyler's actions. We all simply attributed his acts to immaturity. Still, he was always able to gain everyone's attention, most often by talking rather than acting. It was his daily regimen to make fun of those around him—from teachers to overweight classmates, even his own friends—and most of the time it didn't matter if his subjects were present or not.

Tyler wasn't that "bigger than everyone else," "black leather jacket wearing," locker-stuffing bully. In fact, he was so frail-looking I couldn't believe some linebacker or hay bailin' farmer hadn't snapped him in half. Tyler wasn't a neglected child. He didn't come from a bad home. He belonged to a family that loved and cared for him, so I'm not sure why he felt the need to be a psychological terrorizer.

Now, from an adult perspective, as I recall Tyler's behavior, I'm regretful of all the times that I could have defended someone and didn't. I'm ashamed that I never put a stop to the episode at the lunch table. Often, I think of how I could have said or done something to prevent his bullying, but then it had been much harder. Now, I see that I was too consumed in popularity to have taken a stand against his actions.

Although I was confrontational when it came to issues involving me, I didn't always speak up for those in need of support. Like most teenagers, I didn't want to offend or threaten anyone. I just wanted to continue to be accepted, to be everybody's friend. Making my friends or their friends angry would jeopardize my standing among the student body. Throughout high school, I had planned to stay on the good side of those with whom I had had no previous conflicts, which was everyone but the Honeybees. The simple strategy of maintaining constant niceness, even when I disagreed with or disliked someone, safeguarded my position as a well-liked, all-round good-girl.[76]

However, my approach changed when I myself became one of Tyler's victims. My parents promised to handle the e-dilemma. Mom called Tyler's mom, Lisa, to schedule a meeting to talk about the threat. Over the phone, Mom briefly filled Lisa in on what had been happening to me. Unaware and appalled by the Honeybees' actions, Lisa said that she wouldn't blame me if I knocked someone's lights out.

During the meeting, Tyler admitted that he and his friend, Richard, who was also one of my friends, had sent the e-mail. In his confession, Tyler avoided the seriousness of the matter by saying that they had only been joking. After my parents informed him that it's illegal to send threatening e-mails, he became nervous and more willing to correct the matter.

Mom and Dad could have pressed charges. Instead, they agreed to take no legal action and simply asked for apologies. Tyler and Lisa both said sorry, but

Richard's mom, who had also joined the meeting after Tyler had called him out, felt it unnecessary because Richard had denied being involved. I was hurt by Richard's reaction. I felt as if he no longer cared about our friendship, and for that I instantly wrote him out of my life.

Shortly after the meeting, my parents called me to tell me that Tyler was on his way to our house to apologize. At least Tyler was attempting to right his wrong, or maybe he just didn't want to be shipped off to a juvenile detention center. To grant us privacy, Mom and Dad decided to run a few errands before coming home.

As I hung up the phone, the sky released several Civil War-like rumbles. I stepped out on to the porch and judged that the atmosphere was reacting to the tension that would soon arise inside my living room. I was used to the sometimes violent summer storms that occurred in the Midwest, but I wasn't used to the stress that came with the rumbling thunder of this one.

Returning inside, I grabbed the remote, turned off the television, and fell faint-like onto the couch. Lightening flickered above our skylights. I followed the first giant plopping raindrops as they streamed down the glass. After a while, they fell too fast to focus on a single drop. They came inconsistently—in sprinkles, in rivulets, in downpours, then in sprinkles. The thoughts that whipped through my head mimicked the storm's routine.

At first, I wondered what Tyler and I would say to each other and how we would work through the awkwardness. Then the overwhelming fear of losing a close friend invaded me. Things between us might never be normal again.

When I heard Tyler's vehicle pull into the driveway, I went to the door and watched him walk up the sidewalk stiff-armed and tight-fisted. His head tilted toward the cement, but his eyes looked up toward me. I apprehensively said hi, invited him in, and offered him a seat.

"You … probably … know … what I've … come to talk about," he hesitated. I shook my head and sat down on an ottoman, slumped over with my elbows on my knees. As we discussed what had been done, he said sorry and that he never meant for any of it to be such a big ordeal. I accepted but doubted that he and Richard had been the e-mail's only creators. He couldn't answer why they had sent it. He just kept staring at the floor, holding his hands out, palms up, saying, "I don't know." I wasn't convinced. When I asked who else was involved, he admitted that Amber and Chelsea were the masterminds.[77] We were silent for what seemed like an hour, but were only a few minutes.

As the rain lessened, my thoughts came pouring out of me. I told him, "Tyler, you can't let those girls get to you. They don't like me so they're gonna try to drag you into things." After continuing my cliché, don't-give-in-to-peer-pressure, know-who-your-friends-are lecture, I actually thought that I had impacted him. By the way that he kept holding his temples with his palms, I figured that he was contemplating some serious changes. Hopefully, I would never again experience problems with Tyler, and maybe he would even consider treating others with more respect. Unfortunately, it wasn't but a few weeks into our senior year that I noticed my words hadn't impacted him.

Sucker Punched

Finally, in the fall of our senior year, on a Friday morning, homecoming elections took place. Three senior girls would be elected to the court, and whoever had the most votes would be crowned queen. Sitting in my first period study hall, my chest became heavy as I watched the teacher distribute the half sheet, baby blue ballots. The pressure was on. Everyone knew *this* was *it*—the long awaited, final duel between Sara and me.

After about five minutes of silent deliberation, the papers were collected. A group of my male friends gave me fist-pumps and Black Panther-like salutes and told me that I had received their votes. I smiled, grateful but careful not to reveal my excitement.

When the dismissal bell rang, I grew hopeful as I merged my way through the crammed hallways. In passing, many students told me that they had circled my name. Freshmen and sophomore girls bustled to me, tugging my shirt sleeves saying, "You're definitely gonna win."

That night I went to our football game where more students told me the same. With my confidence near maximum altitude, I tried not to look or act too excited. Even if I were to win, acknowledging a victory over the other girls would be improper and would likely result in my being labeled stuck-up. As a female, not only was I supposed to keep my aggression quiet, I was also required to seek out popularity then deny that I was popular and that being popular made me feel good.[78]

As I started the following week, I expected the usual routine, but after I received news that I was selected as a queen candidate along with the Honeybee queen, Sara, and one of her worker bees, I sensed the week would be anything but boring. The final result was already tallied and known by the homecoming advisor and Mr. Littlefield, but the queen wouldn't be announced to the student body and public until the pep rally, which was to be held in approximately two weeks.

After finishing a day of uninteresting classes, I ventured to basketball conditioning then stayed for the volleyball games to take yearbook pictures (I was a yearbook photographer). While the junior varsity team warmed-up, several varsity players approached me. They told me that just minutes before, when they had gone to the water fountain, they had heard Tyler babbling about me to one of his friends, explaining how I had ruined his previous weekend. "Huh?!" I asked, clueless as to what the players were talking about.

I had expected things would never be the same with Tyler and me. We had uncomfortably tried talking in the hallways several times, but we weren't friends like we had been. As a result, I had been out of touch with Tyler's social doings. Tyler had convinced the group at the water fountain that I was responsible for crashing Amber's last Saturday night's party. He told them I had snitched it out to the sheriff and that I had reported to Mr. Littlefield the name of each individual who got busted for drinking, which in turn, caused several football players to be suspended from the team and Sara to be suspended from field hockey and disqualified from the homecoming court.

Up until the volleyball game, I had no idea the party had occurred. Now, all of the sudden, I was thrust into the center of its hype, even though I hadn't been even remotely involved with reporting the incident, and had even been unaware of Sara's ineligibility to participate on the homecoming court.

Eventually, I learned through a public incident report, which my family had obtained from the sheriff's office, that what had actually happened was, on Saturday night, Amber had thrown a party at her house, which led to her being arrested on several accounts: resisting arrest, obstructing official business, and underage consumption of alcohol. Sara, Dawn, and a few other Honeybees weren't arrested, but they were reportedly suspected of underage drinking. The volleyball girls told me that Tyler bragged about not getting caught drinking at the party. He told them he had averted the deputy by sprinting out Amber's back door and jumping over a fence.[79]

The report also stated that it was Amber's next-door neighbor who called the sheriff and that it was standard procedure for the sheriff's office to notify school officials of students' illegal activities. After speaking with deputies, Mr. Littlefield notified a panel of faculty about the situation. The panel then held a meeting where they decided Sara could either step down or they would vote her off. Sara refused to decline, so she was kicked-off, and because she had signed an athletic drug and alcohol contract, she was suspended from the field hockey team. With Sara's downfall, a replacement was obviously needed: the senior girl that had the next greatest amount of votes was to replace her.

I quickly disputed Tyler's outlandish accusations against me, but it didn't matter. Soon the whole volleyball team knew what I had supposedly done. Players came up to me and said, "So I heard you got Sara thrown off court." Others, curious as to why I appeared upset, joined the huddle to get the scoop. It would only take a few hours for the entire school district to hear the tale.

If I had sat down on the bleachers to think things through, I might have realized that I could have easily proven Tyler's story was bogus. It was something that most students probably would have dismissed and forgotten in a couple of weeks—*Or not.*—All I could focus on was how everyone seemed to be thinking the rumor was true, because over the years, the Honeybees had convinced our peers that I hated Sara and that I was engaged in a so-called ruthless competition with her.

Surrounded by volleyball players, my short fuse with the clique sparked and was minutes away from booming. With so much blame placed on me, my skin flushed. I needed to stop the defamation from occurring all over school. It was time to fight for my reputation or risk having it ruined.[80]

My brain started to bang, and my neck tightened as I clenched my teeth. I handed my camera bag to a player and took off running, looking to track-down the rumor-spreader. I figured that Tyler was still at school because he had cross country competition that night. With my arms pumping like sledgehammers, I sprinted out to the football field then stopped to scan the area. Unable to locate Tyler, I kept looking. I searched the practice fields and field house, but he wasn't there. Passing a few people, I asked if they knew where he was, letting everyone within earshot know that I was "gonna kick his ass." When I found him in our gym, playing around with a few teammates, I poked my head through the doorway and asked to speak with him outside. I walked ahead to make sure no one was around, then I assumed my hands-on-hips-head-bobbin'-give-me-an-explanation-now stance.

As I began my confrontation, Tyler's eyes shifted to the ground. He said that he hadn't said anything about me, but I didn't believe him. I demanded to know why he had been talking about me, why he had betrayed me twice. With a crooked grin, he continued to claim that he didn't know why I was so livid. And that's when I socked him under his left eye.

His mouth fell open. His forehead frowned and his eyes widened. He lifted his fingertips to his cheekbone. Unsatisfied with the power I had packed in the punch, I hit him again. He began to cry. He whined, "You hit me … Oh my God, you just hit me." Then he sped off back into the gym.

At that moment, I was pleased with my actions. Surely, through Tyler, I had sent a message to the Honeybees. I knew I couldn't have got physical with any of them, but Tyler was a boy, and boys were supposed to fight.

I marched back into the gym, finding my camera in the bottom row of the bleachers, intending to pick up where I had left off, but before I could put the flash up, Mr. King, one of my basketball coaches, approached me. Like a father preparing to hear yet another lame excuse from his troublesome child, he asked, "Wha'd ya do?" He *already* knew. *Uh*! I thought. *Why did* EVERY*one* know EVERY*thing that happened in my life*!? "He deserved it," I quickly and cockily retorted. Coach King told me that I would probably get in trouble, but I said that I didn't care. It wouldn't be long before Mom and Dad would know what I had done. Wanting to be the first to explain how things went down, I rushed out of the gym to a hallway pay phone and called home.

Mom answered, and I breathlessly rambled through the details, telling her that I had snapped because I was fed-up with the Honeybees' shenanigans. She instructed me to stay away from Tyler and to stay put until she could get to school to settle me down.

When she arrived, I jabbered on, waving my hands in every direction. She fell back against a hallway wall and took a big sigh. She didn't say much. She had seen it coming.

That night, Tyler's mom, Lisa, who once seemed empathetic to what I was going through, threatened to file a complaint with the sheriff's office, and the next morning she met with Mr. Littlefield to inform him of the incident.

That morning at school, I didn't see Tyler, but I heard from a few guys on the basketball team that I had given him a noticeable shiner. When I heard this, I felt proud. I smirked as I mentally replayed the episode. I was certain my actions would be admired by the many who didn't think much of Tyler's funny-man conduct. *Someone's gotta thank me for puttin' him in his place ... for doin' what so many of us wanted to do for so long*, I thought. Sure enough, just minutes into the fourth period of the day, I was recognized ... with a five day out-of-school suspension.

I was somewhat shocked to learn of my punishment. As I sat slumped over in front of Mr. Littlefield's desk, he told me that I had made a bad decision, a mistake that I had to learn from. After everything I had told him about the Honeybees' attacks, I wondered why he acted surprised by my retaliation, as if he had never anticipated that serious problems would arise. "It wasn't the right thing to do," he said as he tilted back in his seat. I dearly wished for him to tip his squeaky 1970s polyester roller chair. His words rhythmically tumbled in my mind like a load of laundry. He might as well have said, "McCandlish, you're a fuck-up. Get the hell out of my office," because *that* was how humiliated I felt. I was infuriated because he had never disciplined or even warned anyone who had bullied me.

Now, I was the only one being punished, all because I had defended myself, and it didn't make sense to me.

Looking back, seven years after receiving my punishment, I finally understand why I was suspended, and I'm finally sorry that I resorted to violence against Tyler. Now, I see that I had physically broken the assault/physical action rule under the serious misconduct code. I had acted irrationally, and I had hurt Tyler. For those things, I deserved to be disciplined and to be taught that violence solved nothing, that it only hurt more people. By suspending me, Mr. Littlefield was simply doing his job, well, at least a portion of it. What he wasn't doing was implementing the psychological harassment/menacing code. I felt that throwing a few punches was justification for Mr. Littlefield's lack of enforcement. But what I felt didn't matter, and it seemed that the reasons behind my aggression didn't matter either.

Mr. Littlefield never questioned why I punched Tyler. Neither did any other administrator or teacher. There was no need. My actions seemed pointless. I had made a noticeable error in judgment and had placed myself in a situation that allowed me to be easily blamed; a situation in which Mr. Littlefield wouldn't have to re-evaluate his part or how our system could better deal with bullying.[81]

My punishment wasn't the only thing that crushed me. Punching Tyler didn't create the response I had anticipated among the student body. Once the Honeybees found out I had been suspended, they took advantage of my absence by advocating Tyler's side of the story. They told our schoolmates that I had no right to act the way I did and that the only reason I had done so was because I wanted to make sure that I won homecoming queen and Sara didn't.[82] On the contrary, hitting Tyler was never about winning homecoming queen. I hit him in an effort to prevent losing my peers' respect and being humiliated by the Honeybees.[83]

The days that followed my suspension foreshadowed miles of turbulence, and I began an abrupt descent. However, the focus of the controversy quickly grew away from the injury that I caused Tyler and became centered on the grief I had supposedly caused to Sara. Instantaneously, I went from "class-act" to "no class."[84]

Having no knowledge of what had been happening to me, many students picked-up on the realignment of power and, because conformity supports safety, they joined the Honeybees in degrading me.[85] Schoolmates, most of whom I thought were friends, took the opportunity to vent about my family and me. They started calling me names of which "rich bitch" became the most common. Ironically, many of these name callers were the same people who, at the beginning of the school year, had voted me "Best Personality" in our class. One class-mate, in front of several students and a counselor, screamed at me in the main hallway. "Getting Sara kicked-off court was something you had no right to do! I hope you get everything you have comin' to you!" she bellowed. The counselor didn't even intervene. He just stared for a couple seconds then turned and walked toward his office. Students also created notebook petitions, intending to have me disqualified. And they said that they would throw things at me while I rode in the homecoming parade. (For protection, Dad and two male friends had to walk beside my car the whole procession).

So many students threatened to vandalize my house that my parents set-up a video camera in our upstairs window. One night, Dad even caught a car idling in our driveway. He chased the trespassers away and followed their car to its final destination—Richard's house. Because it was 2 a.m., and because Dad found out who had been in our driveway and prevented them from causing any destruction, he simply turned his car around and returned home.

Sara's mom even joined the students' efforts in seeing to it that I was pun-ished. She placed a call to Mr. Littlefield and demanded that a re-vote be held and that I be barred from the court. Within only a few days, it seemed as if a handful of envious, frustrated people had destroyed me and invoked uproar in an entire community.[86]

Mom and Dad spoke with Mr. Littlefield who guaranteed that he would do everything possible to insure my safety and see that my situation didn't worsen. Because he had never followed through with his commitments, Mom and Dad were skeptical. In their preparation for potential problems, my parents asked Mr. Littlefield if I had been voted queen, but he wouldn't answer. Mom asked again. *Awkward pause.* His silence seemed to answer Mom's question. He finally responded, saying that even though I had been permitted to remain on the court that it would be best, under the circumstances, to hold another election specifi-cally for homecoming queen. My parents objected but made no headway, leaving them feeling incapable of protecting me and upholding my confidence during my vulnerable emotional state.

As a senior, I didn't understand why a re-election needed to take place. At that time, I didn't recognize that my community's response was part of the universal concept that forbids females from directly displaying anger. Rather, I saw it as a direct attack on my individuality. I felt as if the only reason the re-election was being held was because people were angry at me for supposedly getting Sara kicked off the homecoming court, and they wanted me punished by seeing to it that I was not elected queen.

Now, as an adult, I see how the do-over made sense. In most cases, homecoming queens are respected and admired. They embody everything that an ideal young woman is supposed to be. By societal standards, I no longer met those expectations, and if I were rewarded with a pretty crown, a symbol of elegance, it would most likely cause twice the outrage that had already been created.[87]

No one could explain this to me when I was a senior, though. As a result, my confidence took a whack like a mafia victim. This was the first time that I had to deal with big-time rejection, and I didn't deal with it well. I felt as if I were being double-punished, monumentally shafted. Sole blame had been placed on me, and I wanted to quit, but my parents advised me not to give-in to what so many people wanted me to do, and I agreed. So I remained on the homecoming court, feeling betrayed and abandoned by the people that had put me there in the first place. With an entire weekend of homecoming festivities ahead, I only foresaw my situation worsening. The only way I could cope with being rejected was to start returning the mistreatment to those who had mistreated me.[88]

Dead Girl Walking

A week later, the dreaded day of the crowning captured and consumed me. Somehow, I had made it through eight class periods of near panic and only had one more to go before being suffocated by the weekend's festivities.

Surviving the first event, the pep rally, seemed impossible. Supposedly, I was to be escorted onto the basketball court in front of hundreds of booing students who were going to throw various food items and chant profanity at me. I would rather have braved the pits of Hell than to have entered that scene. Unfortunately, I forced myself to go through with it because I wanted to show that I didn't *need* to be homecoming queen.

As the bell tolled, beginning ninth period, I lurched toward the sweltering gym, shackled by a ball and chain of embarrassment. I found the other attendants and their escorts had excitedly gathered. They were laughing and flirting. One of my escorts, Blaine, had joined them. Having to wait with them for the rally to kick-off was excruciating. None of them would speak to me or look at me, which wasn't surprising because they were all friends with Tyler and the Honeybees. I heard a few of the guys make several inside jokes. By everyone's condescending giggles, I assumed the remarks were about me. Kevin, my other escort, was just as uncomfortable as I was. Trying to conceal our irritation, we turned our backs and acted as if we didn't notice or hear the group.

A few faint voices began floating through the halls beyond the gym. Then, in seconds, a burst of noise rushed upon me like an avalanche. Soon I would be buried, frostbitten, and trapped by my schoolmates' cold stares and icy words. Leaning against a wall, I tensed my muscles, hoping it would lessen my trembling. As the marching band began to play, my pounding heart matched the thump of its drums. With every beat, my abdomen quaked, and my lower lip quivered. I tightly clasped my shaking hands, sure that if I relaxed, the Richter scale would be alerted of record-breaking tremors.

As the gym's occupancy increased, my mind formed the slurs that I was sure my classmates would yell. *Money spendin' bitch. Goodie-goodie's goin' down. Richey-rich spoiled loser. Fuck you Tami! Whore. Snitch. Go to Hell prep. Your fifteen minutes are up!* Everyone would be against me.

Testing … one, screeeeech, two, testing, the microphone screamed, awaking from its slumber disturbed. As the junior attendant was introduced, I snapped out of my production of worst-case scenarios. I closed my eyes, inhaled deeply, and demanded my smile to show itself. The speakers moaned my name. Blaine took off without me.

Two weeks earlier, Blaine and I had held hands and were inches away from our first kiss, which probably would have led to him asking me to be his girlfriend (so I was told by our mutual guy friends). But ever since I had punched Tyler, who was one of Blaine's good friends along with several Honeybees, Blaine had stopped talking to me and started treating me as if I were invisible.

As Blaine, Kevin, and I began our walk onto the basketball court, Blaine moved at least two feet away and a step ahead. I caught a glimpse of his profile. His face was stigmatized with disgust as if to tell everyone that he had been forced at gunpoint to accompany me. I quickened my pace to hold onto Blaine's arm, pulling Kevin into alignment. I can only image that our staggered entrance looked as awkward as it felt. It was recovered when Kevin quickly hopped into place beside me.

The only thing that I wasn't worried about was Kevin being repulsed. If I had felt any amount of security at that moment it came from having him by my side. He was my best guy friend. We were so close we might as well have been brother and sister.

Still, even with Kevin, I was beyond embarrassed. I fought to prevent my inner feelings from making an outer appearance and struggled to hold my closed-mouth smile upward. It twitched when I saw that several boys had turned their backs to my entrance. My chin became heavy, wanting to tilt toward my clavicle. Holding back tears, I blurred the crowded bleachers into a tied-died mess and morphed the noise into a mess of static pitches. I had been on that court before, focusing out rude comments and gestures. Only this time it was far more disheartening, knowing that it wasn't the opposing fans that were against me but my home team.

Finally, all the attendants lined up. I couldn't bring myself to look at any of them. Everyone in the crowd fell silent. I knew my name wouldn't be called, but I was still nervous. I was standing in front of too many infuriated people. I prayed no one would throw anything or, at worst, attack or shoot me.

My tears receded, and I focused my eyes on the crowd, frantically searching for my downsized group of friends. They had been sticking up for me as if it were their job. Naturally, I expected them to be there for me now, but at this point, I felt as if anyone could abandon me. Finding my friends unmoved by the surrounding disorder and looking as if they too wanted to leave the pep rally, I felt a little safer. I yearned for their help, but as badly as I wanted them to save me, I knew there wasn't a damn thing that anyone could do. Again, my eyes watered. Standing at mid-court, I laid to rest the feeling of acceptance.

This was my slaughtering, the court my chopping board, the students my butchers. Everyone could take a slice of me and devour me however they liked— alive, raw, charred, or roasted … And there was my first steak-knife-to-the-stomach spasm.

When one of the other candidate's names was called as queen, the silence was broken for several seconds. The loudest reaction erupted from the middle of the bleachers where the recently expanded Honeybee colony stood. They screamed their woohoos and pumped their fists, looking at me, laughing.

Unsurprised yet still humiliated, I quickly needed to show that this announcement wasn't as important to me as it was to them. Spontaneously, I walked toward the queen and congratulated her with a hug. She stiffened. Others gasped. One boy yelled, "Hit 'er!" Several others said, "Go back to yer place in line," and "Gimme me a break." Every remark slashed its way into my memory and embedded itself into a fresh wound of vengeance.

When the dismissal bell rang, the Honeybees mingled with their queen while the rest of the student body stormed out the doors to the parking lot. A couple of my friends waited with hugs, which only made me feel worse. I hadn't been hugged like that since fifth grade when my grandpa died. Other than the passing of my grandparents, this had been the most devastating loss I had ever experienced, but not because I couldn't take losing. Through sports, I had learned how to lose gracefully, but never before had I been defeated so reprehensibly.

I stayed until the gym nearly emptied. I thought that I would want to sprint out, but I could hardly move. I was petrified that when I turned to leave I would be swarmed by mocking and taunting Honeybees. My friends walked me to the hallway where I reluctantly parted from them to fulfill my decorating duties.

I had absolutely no desire to be festive, but the court was responsible for turning the cafeteria into a '50s sock hop. I thought my presence would show that I hadn't gone home to throw a pity party, and it would prevent at least one gabfest.

Upon entering the cafeteria, I expected everyone to be standing around gossiping, but there were only two other decorators, both of whom ignored my entrance. *Why the hell am I still here?* I wondered. I wasn't going to spend my time and energy at something that I didn't even want to be a part of. My screw-you-because-I-got-screwed attitude erupted. I let a partially inflated balloon fly. It looped its way to the floor, reminding me of my reputation—filled one minute then flattened within seconds.

My life was just beginning to feel as if it were over. I stomped to my car. Fury shot down my leg and squashed my gas pedal. Arriving home, I swerved into our driveway, flinging gravel in every direction. I slammed my brakes, skidded to a stop, and marched straight to my room to scream into my pillow.

Mom and Dad knew what had happened and came to ask if I was okay. I tried to persuade them to allow me to stay home from the game, but they urged me to go, reminding me that my absence was exactly what my bullies wanted. For this reason, I unenthusiastically decided to suck-it-up, and I planned ways to annoy my onlookers.

For a mild start, I complemented my skirt suit and pantyhose with tennis shoes. It wasn't exactly a lady-like appearance and would hopefully irk the conservative crowd. At least I could go to the game looking forward to causing aggravation.

That evening, as soon as I entered the gates of the stadium, I heard comments about my "appalling" outfit, just as I had anticipated. *Can you believe she's wearing tennis shoes!?* a few women asked. But before I could take pleasure in irritating anyone else, I was quickly disgraced. Among five sparkling, white golf carts sat mine, noticeably different. I knew it was mine because the cheerleaders, several of whom were Honeybees, were responsible for cleaning and decorating them. Not only did they assign me the dirtiest cart to ride on around the track, but neither did they decorate it, as they had for all the other attendants. Mom found a cloth and helped me scrub the dust and dried mud off the seat and hang my signs. Unknowingly, the two of us had been booked as pre-game entertainment. I saw that Mom and I drew a crowd of long-distance onlookers who found pleasure in watching us stick-out in a not-so-good way. I tried not to look up at them.

Ten minutes before I was supposed to walk down the field, Blaine stood me up. The homecoming advisor told me that I was prohibited from finding a replacement, which, in my mind, confirmed she was in on Mr. Littlefield's plot to ruin my life. Snowballed, dropped jawed, and speechless, I turned to Mom, who insisted to the advisor that Blaine's place be filled. Everyone else would have two escorts. I would be mortified if I only had one. Like I wasn't already out of place! The advisor refused to change her mind, but Mom, Kevin, and I didn't listen to her objection. Frantically, we located my friend Greg, who was brave enough to fill-in.

As I sat in the golf cart, waiting for the parade to start, I wanted to bail, but I was imprisoned by a royal scam. I was so horrified that I had to go through with it all. People needed to pay for putting me in this situation. I thought about taking control of the wheel and mowing down several targets, but I doubted that a golf cart could create the kind of damage that I wanted to cause. Better images came to mind. I could march up to the press box and spit in Mr. Littlefield's face. Maybe I would barge through the bleachers shoving my middle finger in the faces of Honeybee parents. Then I would torch the entire stadium and escape to the cornfields where I would watch flames swallow slanderers.

Thoughts of retribution stayed with me after the procession started, but instead of appearing as fiery as I felt, I acted nauseatingly sweet. I summoned my fake but believable smile and waved to the jam-packed bleachers while my inner voice repeatedly told the crowd to *fuck-off.* As far as I was concerned, it seemed that every person on the home side had been involved in the pyrotechnic explosion of gossip about me. Peoples' comments about what an awful, undeserving person I was had not only invoked fury within me but also arrogance. I sat with more than proper posture—chest out, chin up, smirk—because I thought that if I showed the crowd my indestructibility through even more confidence they would see that the hateful names they called me and the mean comments they made about me couldn't hurt me.

I maintained the façade as I walked down the field. I don't think I fooled Kevin and Greg, though. They must have felt my heart-pounding tension because they kept whispering, "You're doin' great," "Keep it up," "It's almost over." In the background of their comments the announcer noted my accomplishments and future goals. I longed for him to admit a mistake had been made. I wanted him to tell everyone that I wasn't a horrible person, that I had been sabotaged. My typical teenage, this-is-so-stupid attitude resurfaced big-time. I was sickened that such significance had been placed on a $15 plastic tiara and a short-lived title and that I had actually bought-in to the importance of it all. The ridiculous emphasis made me want that crown more than ever just so I could have broken it in two and stomped on it at mid-field. Instead, I hammed it up for the cameras and winked and waved to my friends in the stands.

Traditionally, the court sat together during the game. This year they were minus an attendant. I was getting sick of pretending, and I wasn't about to sit down and play phony chitchat (the thing girls were expected to do when all they really wanted to do was go-off). It was painstaking enough that I had to walk past their snickers to exit the field. It was time to get the hell outta there, but Mom and Dad felt it necessary to stay until halftime. I could tell that they didn't want to be there anymore than I did. I guess staying was their parental attempt to save me by showing that I really could keep my composure in an uncomfortable setting. I might as well have let someone rip out my fingernails with pliers.

The next day, I loathed having to attend the dance. However, I forced myself to go just because it was another way to show the Honeybees that I wasn't going to be overpowered by them. Reluctantly, I mustered up my thrilled-to-be-here-everything's-fabulous veneer and decided I would only stay for a half-an-hour or so. I was required to at least be present for group photographs and the court's procession on to the dance floor.

Once I was at the dance, the homecoming court march especially made me uneasy. I hadn't been booed in unison yet, so I thought it would surely happen now. Surprisingly, when my name was announced, I only heard about 10 of my friends' deafening cheers. They drowned out anything anyone else had to shout and their support made me smile naturally. I felt comforted knowing that I still had friends. I stopped in mid-procession and arrogantly took a bow to thank them and to show the Honeybees that I wasn't defeated.

Lethal Rejection

After that agonizingly horrid homecoming weekend was finally over, I hoped I would be erased from everyone's shit list; however, months later, I continued to be the topic of household dinner conversations and office and classroom discussions.

I found out because Mom told me that she had walked in on school staff members' talks, and my friends told me about out-of-control classroom slam sessions. Many times I would walk into a chaotic classroom and it seemed as if everyone would stop talking and glare. If I questioned what everyone was talking about or looking at, some boy would make a catlike "rrEEEear." Teachers would act as if they didn't hear or see anything. Instead, they would straighten their desks or hide behind a newspaper. The janitors didn't even seem to come to my defense. Often my defaced picture and any piece of paper containing my name littered the floors of the school. I cringed every time I went to my locker. There, I frequently erased "bitch" or juvenile scribbling, and after the one time that I found "Tami is a bitch," on a bathroom stall, I became too scared to look at walls and surfaces.

I dreaded school. I only had about six months left in my senior year, but even so, I still wished I had been home schooled. After all of Amber's assaults, the e-mail threat, and the nark signs, I had researched the option, but an academic advisor promptly rejected my idea, telling me that because I had put in 12 years at our school, it would be much more satisfying to receive a diploma with our school's name on it. At that time, I could have punched myself for listening to him. I didn't care what school's name was printed on my diploma. I was ashamed it would be ours, though.

Everyday I would roll out of bed with a stiff neck and a headache, not caring if I was late or if I even went. I would bury myself underneath my blankets and stuffed animals, hoping Mom would think that I had already left. I could never make myself flat enough, though. She always noticed. To get me out of bed, she would shake my shoulders or grab a hold of my ankles and pull me out. Sometimes I would hold my breath, pretending to be dead. For some weird reason, I thought if I was convincing enough she would leave me alone. Obviously that never worked, so I would send her out of my room by kicking her.

After finally waking up, forty-five minutes to an hour late, I would bypass my toothbrush, washcloth, and makeup and sluggishly walk straight out the door in my pajamas. With my messy ponytail hidden under a ball cap, I wondered how I would ever make it through the next seven hours.

School really shouldn't have felt that difficult. It wasn't as if I did much. Earlier in the year, four of my classes had been changed to study halls (even though the limit was two) so I wouldn't have to be around the Honeybees. A counselor, who had been aware of the Honeybees' bullying since my junior year, said he would make an "exception" in adjusting my schedule. He made me feel as if I were a pain in his butt, as if protection were only awarded in situations more important than mine. Yet, while my counselor required me to withdraw from several electives that I *really* wanted to take, none of the Honeybees had to drop-out of any of their classes or rearrange their schedules.[89]

Out of the few subjects I was enrolled in, it was impossible to avoid the Honeybees and their friends. Because of them I ended up hating my favorite class, advanced English, which I had taken every year and earned my highest grades.

A recent assignment in that class had been to complete one of several projects pertaining to Shakespeare's *Macbeth*. My family had heard that several boys were going to videotape a re-enacted scene. In the film, they allegedly wore my former little league team's basketball jerseys and a bunch of medals and ribbons to subliminally poke fun at my family. One of the boys boasted to some of my family's friends about how the video would blindside and upset me.

The following day, Dad contacted Mr. Littlefield, who confiscated the video before it could be shown. He said he had watched it and didn't notice anything offensive, but he wouldn't release the film to Dad so he could view it. I was just relieved to hear our teacher announce that our class wouldn't be watching it. I could see the boys' disappointment and was delighted that their plans had been ruined.

After this, my English file was stolen from the advanced English class file cabinet. It was basically like my diary. It contained all of my poetry and free writing in which I had vented about the year's events. I don't know if it was taken by the boys or someone from another class, and neither do I know what it was used for, but its sentimental value couldn't be replaced.

As for the rest of my classes, I stopped studying and turning in a lot of homework. Because I had already been accepted to several colleges, I didn't care whether I maintained my high grade point average, so I let it drop. I also failed four of my five senior proficiency tests because I whizzed through the answers, filing in whatever bubbled letter caught my eye.

My academic performance wasn't the only thing that took a beating. Gradually, my leadership roles were stripped away. Unbeknownst to me, I was relieved of my duty as the secretary of the student council. The advisor and members of the group stopped informing me about scheduled meetings and about what issues were covered in those meetings. The year after I graduated, I received my yearbook, and it confirmed that my role had been replaced when, on the student council page, someone else's name and picture were featured instead of mine. Worse, during my senior year, I wasn't permitted to contribute to my basketball team in the same way I had before.

Upon entering my ninth season, the game had become my primary purpose, prayer, and meditation—my Shangri-La. As a senior, I channeled all my effort into helping lead my team to another state title run. I centered nearly every thought on how we could achieve the honor. However, as our schedule progressed, the peace and fulfillment that basketball had always given me vanished, because most of my teammates joined the Honeybees.

In practices and games, if I was the first one down the court on a fast break, or when I was open for a pass, my teammates would look right through me and wouldn't throw the ball. I would flail around and yell, but they would ignore me and say that they didn't see me. Several times, I left practice in the middle of drills. I would pace around the hallway, steps away from packing up my locker.

There were many times that I nearly stripped off my sweat-soaked jersey and threw it in head coach's face. I blamed him more than my teammates because he never did anything to stop their blatant behavior. At the end of the regular season, I even tried to talk to Coach King about it, but he didn't believe any of my teammates were treating me poorly. He said he didn't want to hear my complaints because the team didn't need any problems going into the state tournament. I wanted to quit so badly, but because I wanted to go on to play basketball in college, I continued to tolerate my teammates. I wanted to prove to collegiate recruiters that I was dedicated to the game, and I feared that if I quit, the college coaches might stop pursuing my abilities.

Off the court, some of my teammates would laugh when they would see me. They would tell others that they thought I was a bossy bitch (I was co-captain), and some of the kids at school talked about how several of my teammates were responsible for stringing toilet paper and cheese puffs throughout my front yard.

Some of our fans' attitudes were equally discouraging. While I was playing, students, and few of my former, graduated teammates, booed at me and hassled me with put-downs. They called me "ball hog," and yelled that I wasn't a team player and couldn't shoot well.

One of the most hurtful times that season occurred on winter athletes' senior night. When I was acknowledged, with my parents, we walked onto the court like all the other athletes and their parents, but we were the only people for whom the cheerleaders and student section didn't applaud or cheer. In fact, applause was minimal in general. The response was hurtful, but really, it didn't come as a surprise to any of us. Even my parents had endured their fair share of relational aggression at sporting events, where students would point and laugh at them or mouth them off.

Maybe the students who bullied my family and me figured that we had enough money to repair physical and emotional damage, but what my peers didn't understand was that the memories that my family and I developed couldn't simply be erased with dollar bills.

Being outcast and losing so many friends was one of the worst parts of being bullied. The rejection caused a bitterness that no amount of money could fix. My chest burned every time I thought about how easy it seemed for friends to cash me in. After homecoming I thought that I had figured out who was and who wasn't faithful, but betrayals were ongoing throughout the entire year. I constantly lost sports buddies, lunch room pals, and "forever" friends to the almighty Honeybees.

Yet, the most lethal rejection was yet to come. Over the past few years, my best guy friend, Kevin, who had also been my escort at homecoming, had talked about how much he enjoyed his rising status, but I never thought much of it. I was just happy that he finally felt good about himself. I had known Kevin for 14 years, and I always felt as if he had low self-esteem. Occasionally, I would try to give him a confidence building pep-talk, but it seemed as if incidents from Kevin's past would forever bother and discourage him.

In grade school, Kevin was branded "the fat kid." On the playground, the popular, athletic boys made fun of his floppy belly. He didn't dare swim without wearing a tee shirt, not even at my family's pool when it was just the two of us. Sometimes he wouldn't even come to my house to swim if another friend was invited.

After his freshman year, Kevin warded off junk food and became more conscious of his appearance. He began working out, playing sports, losing weight, gellin' his hair, and snazzin' up his wardrobe with Abercrombie and American Eagle. Soon enough, Kevin scored a girlfriend, joined the soccer team, and was elected to a leadership position within our class. With his rank on the rise, he was no longer known as my tag-a-long, but because he had spent the majority of the year hushing peoples' negative remarks about me, his reputation had taken a significant blow.

Kevin reaped no popularity benefits by standing up for me. As time went on, he only made people angry and lessened his likeability. Pestered with persistent pressure to uphold his status, Kevin decided to end our eleven-year friendship. In our final conversation, Kevin stood outside the front door of my home, the place that he had frequently referred to as his own home, and told me that he was tired of defending me, that he didn't want to fight with anyone anymore, and that he just wanted to be popular.

If I were a stake being driven into the ground, Kevin's betrayal hammered me deeper than any hit had the entire year. I thought he would always be a significant part of my life. I was sure we would share college experiences (even if we went to different schools), sure he would be a groomsman in my wedding, and sure he would share many Thanksgiving and Christmas dinners with me and my family. I had never pictured life without Kevin, until now.

I was baffled as to why Kevin would want to be a Honeybee. Although he appeared to be "buddying up" to their clique, they still excluded him, as they did with many others. They continually hurt him with insults about how much attention he devoted to his appearance, but they would laugh it off and say they were just joking, and he would play right along. It seemed that they liked him only because they could manipulate him. They knew how hard he had worked to become popular, and if he didn't support their strategies, they would destroy Kevin's popularity just as they had done to mine.[90] I didn't know many 18-year-olds who would sacrifice coolness, but several of my other friends had forfeited popularity, so I didn't understand why Kevin refused to do the same.

This episode, tagged on to the rest of the year's events, floored me. In addition to dizzy spells, which sometimes occurred when I overexerted my body, I lost 25 pounds (most of which was muscle), which was a great deal for my petite 5'2" frame. My pant size dropped from a size five to a baggy three and a comfortable fitting zero, a change which I kept hidden by baggy t-shirts and pajama bottoms. Friends and family always commented on my ashen skin tone, asking, "Are you feeling okay? Because you don't look good." At that point, I looked exactly as I felt—exhausted.

Up until my senior season, I had been my team's fastest player, but now, as hard as I exerted myself, my sprint equaled nothing more than a jog. After games, while my parents mingled, I would lie down on the court with my duffle bag as a pillow and fall asleep until they woke me to leave. Playing ball had always been tiring, especially during AAU when gyms exceeded 100 degrees, but not even in the humid days of summer had I depleted so much energy.

Somehow I would gather enough stamina to go cruisin' around town or out to eat with my three best friends, Bailey, Rylan, and Annie (being with them was one of the only activities that I enjoyed). But other than that, I became introverted and stopped going to school events. That year, I had missed hundreds of athletic competitions, three dances (including prom), the school play, three talent shows, multiple pep rallies, and numerous award ceremonies. Most of my time was spent in my bedroom where I would prop an oversized stuff animal up against my door to restrict entrance. When anyone knocked, they would receive a delayed mumble to go away.

For countless evenings, I would lie cradling a pillow, staring out my window or up at my ceiling, thinking of how I couldn't take school anymore, of how I needed to blast my brains out so I wouldn't have to go. So stressed and deranged by constant thoughts of negativity, I would dig my fingernails into my scalp, pull at the roots of my hair, scream silently, and slam my head and fists into my pillow and mattress. Fatigued by my rhythmic sobs, I would eventually drift asleep, only to toss around in sweat-dampened sheets until the morning's glow seeped through my curtains. In my sleep, I would clench my teeth so tightly that when I awoke I could barely open my mouth. Eventually, I had to get an orthodontic mouthpiece, but, to this present day, the dental problem hasn't been fully corrected.

Mom and Dad tried to persuade me to attend counseling, concerned that I was suicidal, but I refused. I wasn't going to the "loony bin." It would be of no help. There was no doctor who could fix my problems. No adult understood; they just wanted to blame me for everything that had happened.

Actually, my parents were right. I was severely depressed and suicidal, both of which were prevalent in my family.[91] Over half of my relatives had been prescribed anti-depressants at some point in their lives. Cutting was their most common injury of choice. Three of my female relatives were cutters. Plus, my great aunt had ended her life when she shot herself in her chest and head.

Considering my family history, it now seemed as if I was destined to undergo emotional difficulty. Often, I pleaded God to make an oncoming car hit mine head-on or to take my life while I was sleeping. I didn't care whether I lived or died. "Go ahead God; wipe me off the fuckin' face of the earth," I would taunt. If He would do the deed when I least expected it, the pressure of having to do it myself would end. Several times, while driving, my car went off the edge of the road. It wasn't because I told myself, "Okay, this is it. I'm going to kill myself now," but because I was uncontrollably crying and couldn't see where I was going. It actually scared me so much that I readily jerk back onto the asphalt. Still, I continued to beg God to do away with my existence. I became so careless with my life that sometimes, when I would cross our busy road, a 55 mile-per-hour state route, to retrieve our mail, I wouldn't look or stop for oncoming cars. It was that negligence that brought me within four-feet of a screeching pickup truck and forced Mom and my sister to witness a near fatality. This incident scared me too. Unfortunately, it didn't scare me enough to want to live instead of die.

When I became sick of waiting for fate, I was tempted to create my own. On one occasion, I sat on our basement stairs, fixated on the rifles in Dad's cabinet. They weren't loaded, but I imagined that the Internet could provide me with instruction on how to insert a bullet.

I didn't really want to kill myself, though. I just needed a way to feel better again, and death had to be easier and more pleasant than being bullied. Envisioning my afterlife took me away from the callousness of high school. I would think, *people aren't like this in Heaven. If I could just be there everything would be better, happier.* I had even been pleased to think that maybe my death would make the Honeybees feel guilt for the rest of their lives, but after serious consideration, I doubted they would show remorse or admit to the pain they had caused me.

Ultimately, the few advantages of suicide that I could come up with weren't worth it. I cried at the thought of putting my family through the trauma of seeing one of our unfinished basement walls splattered with my blood and brain. I knew that if I had killed myself I would never experience the relief I wanted most.

I had been taught that God had given me life and it wasn't my responsibility to end it whenever I wanted.[92] This teaching lingered throughout my thoughts of termination, and I believe it is what kept me living. Miserably, I carried on, thinking that the bullying must have been God's twisted way of punishing me for feeling good about being popular and enjoying my successes.

Forced by the norm to continue with school, I became one of the 160,000 students that stay home every day for fear of being bullied.[93] After I used up all of my "needed at home" days and illness excuses, I no longer cared whether my absences were excused. At that point, I had missed a total of 33.5 days (double that for all of the undetected times that I ended up skipping). If I couldn't permanently get away, the confinement would soon drive me to insanity.

At minimum, I thought about going on a screaming rampage at school. At maximum, I considered severely injuring people. At lunch, I would mull-over stabbing my bullies in the face with my fork and butter knife or driving my car through the cafeteria windows. Not wanting to take a chance of acting-out my demented impulses, I began withdrawing to the locker room. In the corner of the showers, the same place I used to pray with four of my teammates before every game, and in the stalls, I would quietly weep until I would heave.

There were several times when I was almost discovered in the locker room. Because I didn't want anyone to know why I slipped away, I began sneaking to my car, avoiding the parking lot security cameras and a gym teacher who specialized in busting skippers. The more I escaped unnoticed the less I cared if I was caught. I decided that I would fight off anyone who tried to stop me. My outward display of emotion was long overdue. I didn't want to be there, I wasn't going to be there, and I wasn't afraid to show it.

Defiantly, I would head out to my convertible while waving and cussing at the security camera, giving it the finger. I would pause for a couple of minutes to wipe-off the spit and chewing tobacco that spotted my windows. Then, my vision blurred with tears, I would peel out of the parking lot in a blaze, powdering the surrounding cars with the dust that my tires created.

Tarnished Comfort

My eyes were never dry long. That spring, in our district tournament match, my basketball teammates' feelings splattered the backboards full-force.

Up against a team from a show-no-mercy league, known for its low blows and roughhousing, we trailed by 20 points with less than five minutes left in the last quarter. As each second ticked away, we frantically attempted to narrow the point gap.

During a dead ball, a member of the opposing team intentionally bumped into one of my teammates, Janeen, and snidely asked her, "How do ya like that?" As one of our better players, opponents sometimes gunned for Janeen. When she outplayed her challengers, some girls became frustrated and pushed her. Or when opponents outplayed Janeen, they sometimes displayed their dominance by physically reacting.

I had spent the majority of the last six years with Janeen. She was one teammate and friend who I didn't worry about losing. We had such a strong bond on the court that I was certain Janeen would not betray me. Plus, she had never expressed anger or resentment toward me, or anyone else at that. Janeen was quiet. She mostly kept to herself, only concerned with her athletic and academic obligations.

Knowing how a hard shoulder felt, I was at Janeen's side to defend her. I impudently told the opponent, "Give it a rest. You're winning if you haven't noticed." As I turned to walk away, I was relieved upon hearing the referee whistle a technical foul. I just didn't expect him to be pointing at me.

I was frozen in astonishment. The ref's finger seemed to brush the end of my nose as he passed me to report the "T" to the scorer's table. I was smothered. The call suffocated any opportunity for rebuttal and amplified my chronic humiliation.

Within seconds, the buzzer sounded and a player was substituted for me. As I made my way to the bench, one of my coaches said, in that same irritated father-like tone that Coach King had once used with me, only fumingly escalated, "Why would you do that!?" This coach wasn't the only one who had misinterpreted my action. My teammates used me as a convenient target on which they unleashed their disappointment about losing.

As I sat down in the middle of our bench, the space around me cleared, and my teammates moved to the end. After hearing several mumbled "I can't believe you's," I glanced over my shoulder at the crowd, hoping to locate my parents. I so needed one of their everything-will-be-alright looks, but empathy wasn't what I saw or felt. Instead of seeing Mom and Dad, I only saw a conglomeration of people who I was positive were more interested in gabbing about my inexcusable behavior and despicability.

I looked back to the court in time to hear Kylee, one of my teammates, express her disgust. "I can't wait until you're gone 'cause I can't STAND you," she shrieked. I should have stormed center court and yelled, "Didn't anyone see or hear what *really* happened out here!?" but I was still asphyxiated by silence. I kept stiff in my chair, thinking that it made me less visible. I never would have guessed that I would feel so lousy for sticking up for a friend. I finally understood how my former friends felt when they had defended me.

After the horn sounded and the game ended, we headed to the locker room, where some of my teammates continued to blame me for the loss. A post player's face turned red as she towered over me screaming, "What were you thinking!?" She slammed her palm into a locker. Another voice shouted, "Thanks for ruining our season." I was devastated by their remarks. I too was disappointed our season was over. I had wanted a shot at that state title as badly as everyone else, possibly even more, but for me, much more than the game had been lost.

Upset yet insensate to their criticism, I refused to feel rotten. Again, I unloaded my you-can't-hurt-me disposition, using it to finish my season unshaken. As always, I raised my hand, clasping Coach King's, to form the foundation of our huddle. Only one teammate joined. Everyone else remained at a distance, appearing to be too revolted to touch me. I avoided their coldness, urgently wanting to get our "1–2–3–TEAM" ritualistic chant over, but I wouldn't escape their comments.

"Why'd you do that Tami," yelled Erin, one of our senior players. My pursed lips could no longer contain my muteness. "This is what I get for sticking up for my teammate?!" I burst. No one defended me—not Janeen, not even Coach King. Livid, I jerked my hand out of the puny huddle, snatched my bag, and headed for the door. As I exited, I felt the heat of the girls' angry expressions. I cried, "Screw this school because all it has done is screw me!"

I reluctantly re-entered the gym, which was still very much occupied with fans. Heads turned to examine my distress. *S-h-h-h-it*, I thought. *I can't hide it any longer.* Failing to protect myself with my usual defense mechanism, my shoulders rounded, and my head dropped.

I felt entrapped.
Small.
Vulnerable.
Unwanted.

Unable to hide my anguish from my family, I explained to them what had happened on the court and in the locker room. Dad then tried to talk to my coaches about the treatment I had received. However, without responding, they walked away from the confrontation. As I left the gym, weeping, I walked away too—from one of my last refuges.

The next day, I refused to get out of bed to go to school. I was dismayed by my teammates. I wished I had never cheered so loudly for them, spent so much time with them, or cared so much about them. I certainly didn't want to see them that day or ever again. Instead, I stayed home and prepared to turn in my team duffle bag. Violently cramming it full of every item that displayed my school's name or logo, I zipped up and gave back what few treasured memories I had left.

I was so regretful that I had ever been involved with my team that I decided not to attend the end-of-the-year banquet. I didn't tell anyone of my decision, but, somehow, my teammates found out. Then they held a locker-room meeting where they agreed not to vote for me for any of the year's awards.

For the past two seasons, I had received the "Spirit and Spunk" award, given for my ability to motivate and for the passionate energy that I displayed. Not only had I led our team cheer before every game, I also made signs, banners, CDs, anything that I thought might encourage my teammates and our fans. Finally, as a senior, I worked harder for the recognition than ever because, one, I loved doing it, and, two, it was the last year I had a chance to receive it.

It wasn't just my team that made me feel as if my sweat and devotion had been wasted. Mrs. Reed, an administrator, told me that if I weren't present at the banquet she wouldn't allow me any of the honors I had earned. She said it was a rule, although no one I knew could ever find it in the rulebook. This could have been Mrs. Reed's attempt at reverse psychology; maybe she really wanted to see me rewarded for my time and effort. Regardless of Mrs. Reed's motives, I only saw her ultimatum as more heartlessness. No doubt, it had always been gratifying to earn patches, pins, and prizes, but over the last few months, I had become repulsed by the value placed on such so-called accolades.

Final Farewell

Shortly after my tainted sports season, in April, I was betrayed by two more girl friends, and, as a result, I refused to have anything to do with school.

When I met Melissa in elementary school, she had been a chubby-cheeked, longhaired red-head with thick-lensed glasses. Over the years, her appearance hadn't changed much and neither had her living situation. It appeared that Melissa's family struggled financially, but that never seemed to dampen her light-hearted spirit. In class and at lunch we would cause a ruckus with our breath-stopping laughs. Even after hearing a firm, authoritative "GIRRRLS," we always had difficulty containing ourselves.

Melissa and I hadn't always laughed, though. Throughout middle school and junior high, we had had frequent scuffles. Melissa would barge up to me on the playground and demand to know why I thought she was annoying or why I didn't want to be her friend any longer. I always disputed the accusations, and, eventually, Melissa and I figured out that the consistent falsities were a result of Sara's instigations, which caused Melissa to distrust Sara and place confidence in me.

I hadn't known my other friend, Kara, as long. She had transferred to our school from an East-Coast boarding institution at the beginning of ninth grade. As one of the only African Americans among our student body, she automatically drew attention. Her dark skin wasn't the only thing that got her recognized. She quickly became known as prep and a "richy" because her parents were rumored to be well-off.

At first, I didn't see how Kara would fit in with me and my friends. She had had such a strict upbringing that I assumed our goofy, rambunctious behavior would be too much for her prim and proper demeanor. But her scrunched-nose giggle soon found its place among ours. I don't ever remember having conflicts with her.

Melissa and Kara had guarded me through every clash I had had with the Honeybees. Their loyalty seemed unbreakable, and they displayed their faithfulness by acting as my informants. On assignment to contact me, they jigged and jogged their way through the halls surrounded by a red, siren-like glow. Locating me at my locker, they would alert me of how they had stuck-up for me and whom they had done it to and in front of. When I couldn't be found in the hall-ways, they would execute a note handoff in the classroom, or they would give me a "top-secret" call as soon as they got home.

Melissa and Kara always notified me of the low-down, even when I didn't care to hear it. The two girls knew how to trip my panic switch. They knew that relay-ing information to me about the people I could and couldn't trust kept me slav-ishly dependent on and grateful for their "helpful" attentions.[94] However, I began doubting their sincerity when my best friend, Bailey, told me that Melissa and Kara had called me a "spoiled bitch."

Naturally, I was leery of rumors, especially those regarding others' negative feelings about me. I took everything I heard seriously, especially if the news came from Bailey, because I knew I could trust her. There had been so many times that people had supposedly said something bad about me, and the truth had been confirmed through their actions. Fearing the same outcome would result from Melissa and Kara, I inspected the accuracy of the rumor.

Through all of my confrontations with the Honeybees, I had learned that try-ing to resolve individual disagreements among a group was never productive, so I waited until I got home that evening to confront Melissa and Kara one-on-one over the telephone.

Hesitantly, I dialed Melissa's number first. Epinephrine sped through my limbs. My thoughts quickened, and I was afraid that I might blank when I heard her voice. Her mom answered and quickly directed the call to Melissa. She replied with an upbeat hello, but as soon as I began my inquisition, her tone changed, and she began yelling. She kept yammering that I needed to mind my own business. I realized our no-more-than-four-minute conversation had ended when I heard the dial tone. Her reaction proved to me that what had been said was true.

Impulsively, I double-pressed the talk button and punched in Kara's digits. I couldn't control my infuriated tone. I said, "I know what you and Melissa said about me!" She insisted that they had just been joking and that I shouldn't get so fussy.[95] I snapped, refreshing her of how often I had been called a spoiled bitch by people who hadn't been kidding. This time, I was the first to hang up.

I stared at the receiver. It echoed with cruel ridicule. *Damn them.* I only had a few months of school left, and I was just about to flee when I thought that there wasn't much more that could go wrong.

The next day, in fourth period Business class, Melissa and Kara moved to the other side of the classroom to sit with Sara, Amber, Chelsea, and Dawn. *What-*

ever, I thought. Numb to disloyalty, I turned my back to them and refocused my attention on Bailey, Rylan, and Annie, who sat at the surrounding desks. Only a few minutes later, I whipped back around when I heard Sara, who angrily shouted, "I can't believe she did that!" The Honeybees glared and rolled their eyes at me. Obviously, Melissa and Kara had dispensed enough sweet nectar to create a buzz. I never responded. I was dead to their redundant attacks.

At the front of the classroom, just three feet away from the Honeybees, a newspaper violently snapped open and swallowed our teacher, Mr. Pickett. At that moment, I hated him for not intervening. The crack of Mr. Pickett's newspaper seemed to say that he didn't like the conversation he was hearing, but what angered me more was the way he seemed to hide behind the sports section. I twisted back around in my desk chair. Bailey huffed, aggravated, and told the Honeybees to "shut up." Then my three friends comforted me by talking about how we would run off the football field as soon as we were handed our diplomas.

When class released, I dragged myself down the hall, wondering whether Melissa and Kara had ever really valued our friendship in the first place, or if they had simply used my prior status to maintain a reputable presence. Like Kevin, Melissa and Kara recognized that they had endangered their reputations by remaining my friends. The easiest way for the two girls to discontinue our relationship was to showcase my anger against them, just as Sara had done in middle school and junior high. That way, my breakup with Melissa and Kara would appear to be my fault and would award them enough recognition to smoothly transition to the Honeybee hive. By relating their detestation for me to their new alliance, Melissa and Kara would save themselves from exclusion, regain camaraderie, and most importantly, realign with power and popularity. This strategy seems straightforward, but at the time I didn't recognize that Melissa and Kara were simply trying to remain accepted, because rather than trying to figure out why they had hurt me, I only focused on how hurt I felt.[96]

The same day, when my lunch period began, I was the first to arrive at my regular table. I was astounded that Melissa and Kara sat down with Bailey, Rylan, Annie, and me and acted as though nothing had happened. "Are you kiddin' me!?" I said to no one in particular. I stood up and threw my hands over my head in an I-surrender-like-fashion. "NO. I'm NOT dealin' with this ANYmore," I said, firmly. From my friends' expressions, I knew they could see that my try-to-act-sane-to-get-through-the-day routine had finally ended.

This did it. I had finally heard the last rumor and felt the last bash. As far as I was concerned, I had been betrayed for the last time, and I planned to show everyone that it wasn't going to happen again. This time I wasn't going to slink off to the locker room or rebelliously run out to my car. This time I was permanently exiting.

I marched out of the cafeteria with my eyes shifted to the ceiling and my right arm in the air, yelling, "Now I know why kids bring guns to school." My comment confused a table of skaters and stoners. "What'd she just say?" they asked. Before turning the corner toward the office, I unintentionally made eye contact with the lunch supervisor. He had also heard my comment, and his expression seemed to say, "Thank God the head-case is finally leaving."

I flung open the main door to the lobby of the high school office, bypassed the reception counter, and demanded to the administrative assistants that I speak with Mr. Littlefield. He wasn't present, so Ms. Pinkerton, the vice principal, fulfilled his duties. She led me into his office, circularly rubbing my back. She handed me a tissue and insisted that she knew what I was going through, even though I hadn't told her what had happened with Melissa and Kara or anyone else. Her condolence made my nostrils burn. How could *she* possibly understand what *I* was going through? All she ever did was sit in her office and file paperwork. *She doesn't have a damn clue as to what I've been through*, I thought. As far as I was concerned, no adult had a clue.

After consoling me, Ms. Pinkerton excused me for the day, but I hadn't come to ask for permission to leave. I had come to seize Mr. Littlefield by his tie, jerk him to my furious face, and tell him that I hated him for never helping me.

As I drove home, I bawled the entire way. Traveling on a winding state route, I blinked hard, but my vision couldn't be corrected in time. My tire dropped off the edge, causing my steering wheel to joggle. I closed my eyes, not caring what happened, waiting to screech against the guardrail, but instead of wrecking, my car glided back onto the road.

When I arrived home, I tried to gather enough sanity to make it appear that I had made a strong and sound decision to leave school. Mom was busy in the kitchen, so I stood in front of her at the island bar. Ironically, it had been the same place where, six years before, Sara had implied that she would destroy me if I got in the way of her homecoming goal.

"What are you doin' here?" Mom asked. When I told her that I had left, her motherly concern kicked in. "Do I need to call the school or write a note?" she asked. "You can't keep leaving whenever you want." I wondered if she even noticed my swollen cheekbones and pink tinted eyeballs. She asked why I left, but I didn't answer. I feared she would say the same thing I had heard from everyone else the entire year: "It's just teenage drama. Everyone goes through it. Suck it up." My face got hot. "I'm not going back there!" I yelled, spit flying. "I just wanna die!" I was afraid to look at Mom, so I don't know how she reacted. Instead, I shoved a barstool, stomped to my room, slammed my door, crawled onto my bed, and wailed.

About an hour later, when I had pretended to fall asleep, I heard Mom tiptoe back the hallway. My door brushed the carpet as it cracked opened. When I heard her again, she was on the phone, speaking with Dad, repeatedly asking, "What do we do?" Moments later, after she had hung-up, she placed a second call, though I was unaware to whom.

I lay facedown on my bed for the rest of the afternoon and evening, motionless. Mom called me to dinner but I didn't even flinch. My stomach rumbled as I listened to my family clang their silverware against their salad bowls and plates. I scooted under my sheets and tucked my knees to my chest to help alleviate my pangs, which passed as I drifted into troubled sleep.

During the early morning, I jumped awake. I had had a nightmare. I was back in the gym, and everyone was there. Mr. Littlefield villainously jeered, refusing to ever let me leave school. Enclosed by a circle of classmates, several of Tyler's friends struck me with desk chairs, beat me to the floor, and spit chew on me. Chelsea put her knee to my throat and ripped out chunks of my hair. "You'll never get away from us bitch," Amber cackled. While books battered my face and kicks cracked my ribs, Sara reigned from the top of the bleachers, thoroughly entertained.

Relieved to wake-up, I propped up on my elbow and smoothed back my hair. My hand traveled to the back of my warm, clammy neck and squeezed lightly. My throat was scratchy as if I had been screaming. I reached to my dresser for my water glass, feeling as if I had a 90-proof hangover. Thank God the bad dream was only a dream, but the tortured feeling that accompanied it was so real that I felt it even in my sleep. I kicked-off my comforter and flipped side-to-side a few times until I dozed off again.

I didn't get up until late that afternoon. As I sauntered to the fridge to retrieve the Tropicana jug, Mom entered the kitchen to inform me that she had called my doctor, who advised Mr. Littlefield and my principal to grant me a medical release from school. I shrugged, unexcited and unrelieved. *I don't need those assholes' approval*, I thought. I had already made my decision, and no one was going to change it.

One of the conditions that allowed me to wrap-up the year from home had been to complete my homework through e-mail. However, I never had as much work as my classmates. Throughout April and most of May, only two teachers sent assignments—one from each. I supposed that they were just glad to get rid of me, especially those who didn't send work. I didn't care. I wished the whole year had been that easy.

Another part of the deal was to take finals in the guidance office. Located by a set of main doors, I could hopefully sneak in and out without many people noticing. Not wanting to spend more time there than I had to, I scurried through tests, randomly circling letters and sloppily bullshitting my way through essay questions.

A week later, one of my teachers informed me that I had "overlooked" several sections of her exam. She wanted me to come back to complete the test. "Ha! Come back!?" I said to myself. "She's freakin' crazy." It was enough that relentless, horrific memories kept me psychologically incarcerated to my school.

Every day that I wasn't there was an entire day that I spent obsessing how my life had been destroyed. My senior year was supposed to be the year that, with 130 of my classmate friends, I created some of the fondest moments of my adolescence. Instead, I ended up with only three friends and piercing memories. Thank God for those three friends, though. If I ever smiled or laughed it was because of Bailey, Rylan, and Annie. Their friendship was sacred to me.

To distract ourselves from the pressures of school, Bailey, Rylan, Annie, and I would go cruising around town on the weekends, yelling random things at pedestrians and any driver who had his or her windows rolled down. Sometimes we would find an empty section of the mall parking lot and drive around in circles (not donuts, just fast loops). Sometimes we would drive an hour away, to Columbus, against our parents' permission. And, on the road, we were always on the lookout for cute boys. One of my favorite memories with Rylan and Annie was when we drove around wearing Halloween masks (don't worry … Annie, our driver, only wore a clown wig). At stop lights, we pulled up beside cars and tried to scare people, or we spontaneously danced to our deafening music. I can still picture Rylan bobbing around in her oversized, wolverine mask. We loved to blast our music, sing loudly, and laugh at our silliness until we cried. In the small spaces of our cars, the four of us were provided with at least four or five hours a week in which we didn't have to think about surviving our senior year. We could just be our fancy-free selves.

Bailey, Rylan, Annie, and I never really talked about what I was going through or how it made all of us feel. I'm sure there were times that my friends were just as frustrated as I was, but I wasn't sensitive to those moments. Secretively, I was often aggravated with Bailey, Rylan, and Annie, because I wanted even more support from them. I longed for them to revolt and display how much they resented everyone who caused me to leave. In my honor, they started a food fight on the last day of school, but that seemed to be the height of their rebellion. Knowing they were at school, not retaliating to my satisfaction irked me. I hated when they talked about the excitement of senior events. Not only was I jealous because I wasn't there having fun with my three best friends, I also didn't understand how they could laugh-it-up and enjoy themselves around people who had hurt me. *Didn't they care more about me than that!?* I wondered. I felt as if they were actually relieved that I had left school. All of a sudden, they were carefree and happy again, and I didn't understand their emotions, because I was still miserable. It was most upsetting to hear them discuss senior breakfast and graduation rehearsal and commencement, because, after spending so many years excitedly looking forward to the celebration, I chose not to participate. No way did I want to spend what was supposed to be a day of happiness with people I hated, feeling hated.

After I left school, I much rather preferred that the only thing Bailey, Rylan, and Annie told me about was the ongoing drama among my classmates. I liked hearing about their falling-outs because I felt as if they were experiencing a little bit of what I experienced. What amused me the most, yet at the same time left me wanting to vomit, was how the Honeybees began to think of themselves as sufferers. Annie told me that they said things like, "I can't wait to get out of this hell hole and away from *these* people," and, "I'm *never* coming back." And their parents told other parents, who in turn told my parents, "I can't wait until my kids are out of *that* school." Despite the Honeybees' rift, at least they could go out in true senior style. They could take that prestigious stroll across the stage without being booed or hissed, receive applaud from the audience, and pose for photographs with their friends and family afterward. I could not, even if I wanted to.

Two weeks before graduation, Mr. Littlefield told me that I had to write a note, declining my involvement in commencement exercises, or he would withhold my diploma. However, I knew another student who didn't end up attending; he didn't have to write a note, and he still received his diploma. Mr. Littlefield also said that in order to make my graduation official, I needed to come to school, before the day of graduation, to have individual photographs taken. *Why couldn't he just mail me the damn thing?* I thought. I refused to go, but my parents insisted, saying they would be sad if they didn't have any cap-and-gown memories to look back on, and they even tried to convince me that I would be sad too. Now, I understand that such events are prideful for parents, but then I wanted no one, not even my mom and dad, to have any recollection of my connection to the school. However, because I wanted to finally rid myself of the place, I grudgingly followed through with instructions one last time, hoping it would all quickly come to an end.

In place of participating in the regular ceremony, I was to meet the presenter of my diploma, Mr. Wilcox, another school official, while classes were still in session. Mom accompanied me for support and probably to make sure I didn't mouth-off too badly. I felt ridiculous, walking around in my bright red cap and gown. I stood out like a cherry in an empty sundae dish. They might as well have dressed me in a clown costume and sold tickets for people to come honk my red squeaker nose. I could almost hear the "Circus Polka" streaming over the loudspeakers.

Mom and I waited in the gym for Mr. Wilcox to arrive as the photographer fiddled with his camera settings. Annoyed, I crossed my arms and rolled my eyes at his every move. Finally, Mr. Wilcox walked in, and the photographer readily intervened. "OhhKaayyy … Stand here … a little to your left … Can we get a handshake … There we go, hhoold it," he said. *Hurry the hell up,* I screamed inside. As the flash fired, I was paranoid that my classmates might flood in melodically repeating, "Gotcha." The entire year had felt like an awful practical joke, and it wouldn't have surprised me if I had been put through it just for the Honeybees' entertainment.

With one painstaking scene completed, there was just another to go. When we arrived at the football field, we once again waited for the fidgeting cameraman to adjust his settings. In the meantime, Mr. Wilcox asked me more questions than I felt like answering. "Where are you going to college? What are you going to study? How's their basketball program?" he asked. *Who's he tryin' to fool?* I thought. *He doesn't care.* His enthusiastic pose seemed to say that he was beaming with pride, as if he had provided so much guidance and support to me throughout my career. But I had barely seen him all year and was angry that he hadn't used his authority to put a stop to the Honeybees' bullying.

When the affair was finally over, the three of us parted from the photographer and walked toward the school. I didn't want to walk with Mr. Wilcox, but he wouldn't leave me alone. He patted my shoulder and looked at me with an unconvincing I-feel-for-ya-kid expression. "Between you and me," he said in a hushed tone, "Tyler got what he deserved," referring to my punching him at the beginning of the year. Irritated, I felt like giving him a few "between you and me" comments. Instead, I tucked my diploma under my arm, climbed into our Dodge Ram, and quietly cursed Mr. Wilcox and every brick of that building to Hell.

◆   ◆   ◆

I thought that renouncing my school meant that I was emotionally over being bullied, but when I returned to school several weeks later, I was refreshed of how not-over it I really was.

It was a pleasant Sunday evening in June. Orange rays radiated a pinkish-blue sunset. I was the only person at the school. I had returned to run on the track because it was a close, convenient place that allowed me to measure distance as I conditioned for college basketball.

As soon as I trotted onto the crumb rubber track, I felt as if someone lassoed my legs to one of the posts of the shelter house. Struggling to maintain a jog, I stopped after my second lap. I was overcome by regret. *Why did I come back here!?* I questioned. In being away for a while, I had somehow forgotten how much the facility repulsed me. I stomped my feet on the inner lane and beat-down the air with my fists. I walked across the field and sat down at the 40-yard line, trying to figure out the purpose of my visit by envisioning past events.

I had had so many happy, memorable moments on and around that field. The first memory I thought of came when I saw the victory bell. My friends and I, with painted faces, had stormed the field and rung it after the football team won its last game of the '99 season. Glancing toward the hill by the field house, I saw my sixth grade boyfriend and me sharing our first kiss. There was my chalk mark on the light pole. I had jumped higher than any other girl in my wellness class, even a six-footer. I was winded as I came out of the cornfields. I had just finished one of my many runs on the cross-country loop. Lastly, I looked toward the soft-ball diamond and saw the spot where a ball had popped up and bloodied my nose. My doctor had said that it wasn't broken, but I could have sworn it was because I had blacked out and bawled. That incident had scared and scarred me so badly that I quit softball.

Sitting on the turf that summer evening, recollecting my school days, I felt that same busted, ruined feeling. I cried, bothered by every memory. "Why did I even go here?" I sadly muttered. I had embedded my youthful presence among so many people, in the soil of the fields, in the stench of the locker rooms, in the torn vinyl bus seat cushions, even on the lunch trays. I was just as much a part of it as it was a part of me. I could never be rid of it. What had *any* of it ever been for? *Pure punishment*, I concluded. I dug my fingers into the soft ground and ripped up sod clumps. Furiously, I rushed to my car, spit on the pavement, screamed through clamped teeth, "I hate this place," and kicked a rusted 50-gallon drum trashcan. I vowed to *never* return.

Grounded

That day, I made sure that I wouldn't forget how miserable I had been at school, but preserving the memory didn't prevent bullying from occurring throughout the following summer and even years after.

The summer after my senior year, the new rumor was that I was a high school dropout. "She must be pregnant," a few mothers said. People never stopped gossiping. They remained disgusted and appalled at my actions. Adults continued to tell mutual family friends that I had no right to act the way that I did. Students in my sister's class, who I didn't even know because they were six to seven years younger, said that I was "mean." After standing up to one of her schoolmates, my sister was told that she was a "snot" just like her sister. Often, my parents received dirty looks from my bullies' parents, some of whom had been long-time friends. And while driving, my family and I would get gagged at or flipped off by my former classmates.

During the year, I was unaware as to how the bullying had impacted my family. It wasn't until four years after my experience that Mom told me she had been prescribed Prozac. She would often imagine encountering Sara, Amber, or Chelsea in a secluded place and beating each one of them to near death. My sister visualized the same types of aggressive scenes, motivated by the cries that seeped through our paper-thin bedroom wall. Dad became so frustrated by failed attempts to resolve my problems, and I became so angry at his inability to do so that we barely spoke.

I didn't understand how people could treat my family, especially my parents, the same way that they treated me. Mom and Dad had opened their home, hearts, and cupboards to my classmates. They had thrown many birthday, pool, and Halloween parties for my friends and me. Both had volunteered much of their time to my basketball team. Dad had been a coach, and Mom filmed games and organized pre-game meals in our home.

My parents, like me, became cold toward the school. Mom only returned to drop-off and pick-up my sister. Dad occasionally attended a football or basketball game to watch someone that he used to coach, but he would stand or sit with the opposing team, although I didn't understand how he could even set foot on school property.

While my family shared many of my emotions, I didn't always recognize their feelings. They never appeared as angry as I would have liked. It seemed as if they had instantly and easily forgotten about everything and expected me to do the same. I became annoyed with hearing my parents' "be strong" lectures. They always encouraged me not to let others know that they had bothered me. They said that I simply had to move on, get over it, and ignore peoples' comments and dirty looks. Their suggestions led to many arguments because I wasn't finished being angry. I had just started showing people how much I detested them, and I wished for my family to do the same.

Out of everyone who had bullied me, only one offender expressed remorse. After the end of my basketball season, I received, via mail, a written apology from my teammate Erin. At that time, I was so infuriated that I didn't take her seriously. I wrote back, telling Erin that she had only apologized because of her self-centered, guilty conscience, not because she actually cared about me.

After school ended, Erin, Janeen, and another teammate showed up uninvited to my graduation party. I never saw or spoke to the girls before Dad told them to leave, so I don't know if they came to apologize or to antagonize. If they were there to say sorry, I wouldn't have accepted. If I had received any other apologies I wouldn't have accepted them either. My animosity wouldn't allow it.

I had been hurt by so many people that the effects of bullying seemed permanent. No one could pry open or break through my iciness. Sometimes people would try to crack through, but I was too hard to be penetrated. I had no respect for their attempts at communicating with me. As far as I was concerned, no one deserved my attention because *everyone* had hurt me, directly or indirectly. Each person was connected with someone who had said something, and I was convinced nothing positive ever resulted from anyone's conversations. Because of this, I wanted to show people how it felt to be humiliated.

Sometimes, when I saw people from my school district in a grocery or department store, they would say "hi" and ask me how I had been, and I would just stare through them, trying with my mind's eye to thrust what I considered to be their fakeness into another realm.

At first, when I would spot someone I hated, my hands would start shaking, and I would want to march up to them and tell them off. I never did, though, and the excitement of scolding them always died down quickly. It was dissatisfying to work so vigorously only to finish unfulfilled. The frequent emptiness that was created made me worry about running into familiar people, so I stopped going to local places. I refused to dine in most of the restaurants, and I even boy-cotted the mall. If I had to go anywhere by myself, I took back-roads, and if I shopped, I would drive hours away just to lessen the chances of seeing familiar faces. I only went into town (which wasn't often) when accompanied by my fam-ily. With them, I felt protected, because together we could lash out at our ene-mies.

Community members weren't the only people that I rejected. I also renounced the entire female gender. I told everyone, "I can't stand girls. I hate them." Other than Bailey, Rylan, Annie, Mom, and my sister, I was convinced that all females were harsh, untrustworthy, vindictive, and evil. I was suspicious of everyone's actions but more so every *female's* actions. Therefore, having rela-tionships with them was pointless and hopeless.[97]

If *only* I were a guy. If *only* I could have changed my identity in *some* way, life might have been a little easier, but I never had the nerve. For a while, I was hell-bent on dying my hair hot pink like Gwen Stefani, the lead singer of *No Doubt*. Once, I tried to Clorox my hair, but I chickened out when I heard it sizzle. On another occasion, I cut a four-inch chunk out of my hair. Really, I liked my long, dishwater blonde hair. It was one of my trademarks and what everyone knew me for, but I was sick of being known in my community. I thought if I could alter my physical image it might de-emphasize my bad-girl reputation. However, to my disappointment, I couldn't find any way out of my perceived identity.

While I had attempted to detach myself from my hometown and half of soci-ety, it seemed impossible to do the same with God. Even though I hadn't attended church in nearly seven years, I still couldn't distance myself from God's presence. He was the one authority figure who I just couldn't snub. Like all adults, it seemed that He wasn't willing to help me out of my predicament, but unlike all adults, He kept nagging at my conscience to tell Him how I felt. He reminded me of a leg hugging, why-why-why asking four-year-old. He just wouldn't let-up, and His persistence aggravated me. I would shake my hands at Him as if trying to strangle Him for constantly resurfacing in my thoughts, but as irritated as I was, I acknowledged God more often than not.

God became the primary outlet on which I vented my anger and placed my blame. I would tell Him that if He really loved me He wouldn't have trapped me in such an awful place with such horrible people. Confused as to why He had cre-ated my unpleasant situation, I constantly demanded to know the reasons for being bullied. I didn't deserve to be chastised. I wasn't a bad person. Sure, I had made mistakes, but it wasn't as if I had murdered anyone. Fed-up with what I thought was God's lack of response, I insisted that He leave me alone, that He leave me to be grounded by pain, but that just wouldn't happen.

Because I wasn't making much progress after I finished school, my parents, once again, asked me to go to counseling. I still didn't want to go. I was stubborn and embarrassed, because I thought going meant admitting that the Honeybees had defeated me. However, after I learned that my parents were considering filing a lawsuit against my school, I gave in.

A week earlier, Mom and Dad had met with two representatives from my school district to discuss a letter Mom had written to the school board. In it, Mom expressed her disappointment with the school's reluctance to prevent bullying. However, the representatives said that the administrators had no knowledge of the problems I had experienced. The representatives apologized for what I had gone through then smugly said that my being bullied didn't cause the school system to fear punishment or litigation.

When I heard that the meeting was unproductive, I finally agreed to see a professional. I was hopeful that the decision would help us win the court case, and, in turn, expose my school's negligence and destroy its reputation—just like mine had been destroyed.

Purpose in Pain

The top of my steering wheel was moist. I had been rubbing my sweating, shaking hands over it at each red light. Every time Mom and Dad had mentioned counseling, I had straight-up refused. I had already asked for assistance, way back before my situation got bad. Now, the chance for help had arrived too late. I was poisoned by unremitting frames of harrowing memories, which no psychiatrist could ever erase.

When I finally agreed to counseling, I did so swearing that I would not engage in chaise lounge sob sessions about my feelings and recurring nightmares. Instead, I planned to control the discussion by adamantly sticking to the hard facts that were necessary to prove my mental and physical collapse to a judge.

On the morning of my first appointment, I had left my house defiant, but by the time I pulled into the counseling center's parking lot, I cowered. As I snuck out of my car, I lowered my head and pulled my hat-bill down, fearing someone would recognize me. My cheeks were sore with tears.

Entering the waiting room, I rounded my shoulders to make my quivering chest less noticeable. Avoiding eye contact with the receptionist, I signed in then sat down in an uncomfortable wooden chair. The hard seat made me think of my school's desk chairs. Unfortunately, everything made me think of something related to school. Not even ten minutes into my wait, I already had numb-butt. This appointment was bound to suck; the confirming indicator—end tables and magazine racks lined with outdated issues of gossip-filled *People Magazine* and *US Weekly*.

When my name was called, I gathered my emotions and followed Dr. Sheridan into her un-doctor-like office where I was surrounded by framed photographs, dream catchers, and figurine-occupied bookshelves. For a minute or so, my eyes kept busy, and my mind wandered from the purpose of the visit.

Relieved not to find any "entertainment" magazines like those in the waiting room, I cautiously squatted into a recliner, thinking maybe counseling would not be so bad. However, as I sat in silence, watching Dr. Sheridan's pen strokes decorate my paperwork, nervousness thumped through my bloodstream. I pressed my back into the channeled padding of the chair, hoping it would swallow me into its frame and spit me out on my bed at home. Consumed with thoughts of worry, I speculated what awful words she was writing to describe me, and I imagined that as soon as I began testifying she would accuse me of lying.

I was cuss words away from defending myself when my visualizations were interrupted by a soft, "Okay ... So tell me why you're here." *UhHh*! *What nerve! She's already trying to manipulate me!* I thought. She knew why I was here. Mom and my doctor had already called and given the reasons for my visit. I knew what Dr. Sheridan was up to. She was nonchalantly trying to get information out of me so she could use it against me; it was simply ritualistic female practice.

I was too experienced to be fooled by her deceptiveness. Several times, I refused to tell her anything, but she just smiled and persisted in trying to get me to talk to her. After ten minutes, I guessed I was not going to persuade her to lay-off, so I began, pissed and guarded. Though there was something about her expression, a blend of condolence and curiosity that compelled me to spill more than just school absence and weight loss statistics.

Shortly after I began my story, my inflexible game-face contorted, and Dr. Sheridan got up from her chair to hand me a box of tissues. Over the course of two hours, she interrupted only to clarify who was who and who did what. Mostly, she listened quietly, which surprised me because most adults always chimed in with a non-insightful lecture.

During my next four sessions, I was stirred by the loudness of Dr. Sheridan's silence. Her muteness made me aware of the potency of my tone and words. Through it, I heard myself conveying that I was angriest not that I had been treated badly, but at *why* I had been treated badly—why God had allowed such badness to happen to me. All I could think about was *why me ... Why ... Why* did *this* happen to *me*!? Unable to see past my absorption, I became hung-up with the unexplained.

It was during my last appointment that Dr. Sheridan finally spoke. "It seems as if there's a spiritual void in your life," she said. "Void?" I retorted. I shrugged my shoulders in annoyance. I was insulted by the idea. *Here it comes,* I thought. *Another person who feels obligated to point-out what they think is wrong with me.* Yet, there was no finger-pointing from Dr. Sheridan, and after our meeting concluded, I realized her suggestion was simply a reflection of my words. For this reason, instead of taking permanent offense, I stocked the thought so I could think about it on my own.

After my final counseling session concluded, I still did not know how to deal with girls like the Honeybees. Dr. Sheridan had agreed the Honeybees had treated me meanly, but she never suggested that what I had experienced was relational aggression. My current perspective is that Dr. Sheridan was not educated about female bullying, and as a result, she could not pinpoint why the Honeybees had bullied me. Instead, she simply gave me the usual "they're jealous" response and left me to figure out how to deal with future mean-girl behavior on my own, but, as an angry 18-year-old, I was not interested in receiving solutions. I simply wanted an uncritical adult want to hear my story and let me tell my story. Dr. Sheridan had done this. Even so, I had not told her everything. I was relieved to have concealed most of my emotions. I was thankful that I had not had to talk to her about my scratched, scabbed scalp, my weight or energy loss, or about how I daydreamed of stabbing my bullies in their hearts and driving my car off a cliff. I felt embarrassed about these things, and I never wanted to talk to my family, friends, or counselor about these issues, because I believed they would think I was screwed up beyond repair. Yet, even with hateful emotion still festering inside, counseling had stirred questions within me.

Through simply telling my story to Dr. Sheridan, I realized just how incomplete I felt. I spent weeks questioning who I was and who I was meant to become, and the longer I questioned my identity, the guiltier I grew. Maybe my peers were right; maybe I *really* was a bad person. What felt even worse was being so angry at God for having allowed the Honeybees to bully me. I had been taught that it was wrong to be angry at God, and because of this I was left with a shame that freaked me out and followed me like an eerie, lurking, trench-coat-wearing stalker. I could not shake the feeling, and if I did not resolve it soon, I was convinced I would end up in a body cast or a body bag.

I heard about accidental injuries and deaths all the time on television news stories. While authorities expended time and resources searching for the causes of these seemingly unexplainable tragedies, I knew the answers. Back then, I thought that when people were as angry with God as I was, they increased their likelihood of having their car's brakes go out while traveling downhill or being bitten by a virus carrying mosquito. Although over the last year I had often wished for death, I was frightened by the thought of ending up in a hospital or morgue. I was terrified of God's chastisement. For some unrevealed reason, I believed He had punished me the entire school year and that if I did not stop rebelling against Him, He would continue to punish me. Needless to say, I started praying more frequently.

After I had scared myself into begging for mercy, I realized God did not want to ruin my life or do away with my existence. He wanted to build me up and make me stronger, just like it said He would in the books of Jeremiah and 1 Peter.

I will build you up again and you will be rebuilt. (Jeremiah 31:4)

And the God of all grace, who called you to his eternal glory in Christ, after you have suffered a little while, will himself restore you and make you strong, firm, and steadfast. (1 Peter 5:10)

Verses like these made me certain God would bring back my zest, but I was not into waiting for His intervention. I insisted that explanations be delivered immediately.

Eventually, through my desperate pleas, I felt from God the same expression that I had seen on Dr. Sheridan's face, the same expression that told me He was not against me but for me. Right away, He replaced her as my always-on-call therapist.

I figured if I requested God to give me answers I would find wholeness and relief from my problems, but months of praying passed, and none of the things that I asked for happened. My family still had not gone back to church, I still did not understand why I had been bullied, and God had not given any of the Honeybees the consequences I felt they deserved. When results did not turn up, praying seemed useless. Yet, I continued to do it.

Even seemingly more useless, I was expecting God to answer my irrational orders. My prayers were not effective because they were not aligned with my needs, only my emotions. My prayers were echoes of misplaced self-appreciation and angry complacency. In directing most of them toward my family, I had taken focus off myself and placed it on them. I thought that if I prayed for my family to get through all of the drama that they would be able to provide me with spiritual intervention and direction. My family could not help me, though. They had already tried, and I had forbidden them.

My condition would not improve until I became spiritually dependent on God rather than people, but God wasn't going to tap me with some quick-fix, bad-memory-be-gone supernatural stick that would make life presto-chango better. In order to alter my outlook, I understood that I had to practice faith. So, in a self-motivated effort to rework my character, I refocused how I prayed, what I prayed about, and who I prayed for.

This change wasn't easy or automatic. It required a lot of time and effort, just like my basketball foul shots. If I missed more than two, I would shoot 50 to 100 more. It did not matter if it was getting dark, if Mom called me in for dinner, or if my coaches wanted to turn off the lights in the gym. I could not be distracted. I *had* to master my mental concentration when I was shaken by distraction and fatigue.

Like my foul shots, my prayers needed passionate consistency, which could only be attained by developing my own personal approach, adapted to my feelings, personality, and circumstances. For so long, I had robotically followed others' ways of relating to God. Since childhood, I had prayed because adults told me to, because I thought it would keep me out of trouble and stop unfortunate things from happening to me.

Before I fell asleep every night, I would systematically clasp my hands, close my eyes, bow my head, and emotionlessly repeat the "Oh now I lay me down to sleep" rhyme. In an attempt to break away from my usual bedtime manner, I started speaking to God throughout the day with open eyes and expressive body language, just as I had with Dr. Sheridan. It was during the day that I needed God most, because it was then that I struggled with consecutive hours of emotional inconsistencies. Some days, I would only say a few sentences. Some days, I would gush with secrets that I did not even know were within me.[98] Then, there were times I did not feel like saying anything, and I didn't.

My pleas were small but significant. Sometimes I would ask God, "Please don't let me feel this way," or simply, "Help me." Each statement or question drew me nearer to relief because I was able to gain a much needed confidant. Instead of writing God off as I had done before, I begged that He would continue to help me. He was not that adult or friend who told me to forget about everything. In fact, it was as if He forced me to remember what I had been through so I could talk to Him about how I felt. He listened as no one else had listened. His silence spoke through my words, allowing me to liberate my negative energies and reduce the strength of my hatred.

My trusting in God more than myself or anyone else would begin the restoration of my solidity. It would be key in recovering my composure, but not before it forced me to admit some of my faults and my need for God's help. Having to accept that I had been too weak to prevent people from hurting and destroying my reputation was demolishing to my pride. Pride had upheld me and showed people that they could not make me feel awful. Although it felt impossible, releasing my self-reliant strength and taking hold of God-dependent power would be the only way that I would regain my identity. However, when my parents told me that they decided not to sue my school district, I became infuriated. I was sure that since I had made a few religious modifications, God would reward me with retribution by exploiting my school's negligence, but now there was no chance of that happening. I felt betrayed again, as if Mom and Dad had used the idea to trick me into attending counseling.

At the time, I did not understand my parents' reasoning not to follow through with litigation. They tried to explain to me that they feared losing money fighting a court battle and thought it might make future problems for my sister, who remained in the school district. They said that my leaving school had been the easiest way to begin putting my senior year behind us. Their philosophy was that it would be better for our family to try to forget our hurt instead of prolonging it. Now, I see that, like most parents, they only wanted for their children the best outcome that offered the quickest solution and least pain, but, to me, it appeared that they had surrendered too easily and too soon. Without their help in destroying my school's reputation, I promised to single-handedly brawl until I fixed my problems and everyone who had caused them.

After this, I discarded the spiritual progress I had made and became reabsorbed with my vengeful mission. Once again, I became apathetic to guidance. For years after, I would remain too impatient and bullheaded to recognize that I was only prayers away from discovering purpose in my pain.

Seeking a Remedy

As the summer neared its end, I prepared to leave home for college. Although my small university was only a couple hours from home, no one from high school would be going there. In the absence of my former classmates, I thought I would finally be able to escape ruin and renew my reputation. Yet, after just a few bright thoughts, my vision was clouded by uneasiness.

I was terrified about leaving for college, because I had no idea how I was going to survive in a cramped, all-girl dorm room. There was no way that living with females could provide the same security that I had received from the enclosure of my bedroom. It just couldn't be done. Girls just wouldn't allow it. They could be so sensitive and overreacting. With females, the most trivial incident or even the most levelheaded confrontation could launch a recreation of my senior year of high school.

What if I simply asked my roommates to lower their noise level, or to clean up after themselves, or to give me a little privacy? What if they wouldn't share the television? What if we wanted to date the same guy? What if they never went to class and stunk-up our room with weed? What if I said "no" to their actions or lifestyles? What if I had to deal with *another* Sara, or multiple Sara's, or a brand new group of Honeybees!?

I came up with countless reasons that might bring out our differences and cause my roommates to take me the wrong way or to feel threatened or aggressive, and if this were the case, peer manipulation would surely follow. I just knew they would twist and embellish the facts of what I said or did to make others believe that I was a problem-causing bitch.

What if their resentment of or irritation with me provoked them to flat-out ignore me? How could I live comfortably with people I couldn't even communicate with? What if they caused my floormates and classmates to disregard me too? What if they talked badly about me to all of the guys? What if, because of the girls, no one wanted anything to do with me!? I would have to eat lunch and dinner alone. I wouldn't have anyone to hang out with. What would I do with my downtime? Pretend to study? As if that wouldn't make me feel like a loser. I could see myself ending up as the loneliest, most pathetic person on campus.

What if I accidentally angered my roommates so badly that they wrote me mean notes and left them for me everyday before they went to class? What if they scrubbed the toilet with my toothbrush or stole my belongings to make a profit on Ebay? What if they destroyed my computer files or hid my books, homework, or term papers? What if they did stuff to me in my sleep? They might give me a black permanent marker mustache, or chop-off my hair, or smother me with a pillow!

The more scenarios I came up with, the less I considered relational aggression as a "what-if." It was bound to happen, and I prophesized its certainty. College wouldn't be a place for me to rebuild. It would be another battle zone of cruel laughs, looks, and lies, a social warfront where I would be wounded or killed if I put up a fight.

Despite all my trepidations, Dad took me to campus to help me move into my dorm room (Mom couldn't come because she had a broken ankle). When we arrived, and I met my new roommates, I tried not to be overly genial or talkative. I kept my head down, concentrating on helping Dad assemble items and organize my space. Though after everything was stuffed, stacked, and taped in its proper place, and Dad left me to fend for myself, I couldn't help but to warm-up to my new roommates, Maria and Katie. My response to their inquiries about my portion of the room engaged us in what became consecutive evenings of many lengthy get-to-know-you talks. In every conversation hereafter, I discovered our commonalities, and, little by little, my fear of being rejected and treated poorly began to disintegrate.

Over the first couple of weeks, having roommates wasn't anything like I had previously thought. Contrary to my original concerns, Maria and Katie weren't out to tear me apart and make my life hell. I wasn't annoyed or offended by them. Nor was I eating meals by myself, or fighting for bathroom time or closet space. To my surprise, my roommates and I had much in common, and a few weeks later, when Liz was added to our suite in order to fill a vacancy, our bond was further enhanced.

Throughout our first semester, the four of us did all of the "girly" things that I had missed doing with so many of my former friends. We went shopping. We swapped clothes. We scoped out guys. We danced and sang loudly around our room, and we decorated to celebrate each other's birthdays and aced exams. Through numerous late-night laughing attacks and secret-sharing sessions, I paid less and less attention to shielding my heart and openly welcomed and treasured the feminine energy that connected us.

Living with girls wasn't the chaotic mess I had predicted. The contrasting circumstance brought forth a comfort and trust that reminded me girls really could be affectionate and that meaningful, intimate relationships with them weren't unattainable. Yet, it wasn't just the fellowship that I formed with my roommates but also with my new teammates that made me re-evaluate females and pursue friendships with more of them.

Fixated on the memory of how my last basketball season had ended, I was afraid that my new teammates might pick up where my old teammates left off. The worry almost made me forget how rewarding it could feel to be part of an athletic program, but that sweet gratification came rushing back upon my first meeting with my new team.

After a few weeks into fall semester, the girls were reunited as a team for the first time since the previous year. They were full of high-fives and hugs, happy not just to return as teammates but as friends. And it didn't take long before I was officially one of them, as I was presented with a nickname and invited to go along to soccer and football games. I gladly accepted every opportunity to find my place among them, hoping that I too could get through the next couple of seasons with high-fives and hugs instead of harsh words.

Being with my teammates not only added to the camaraderie that I greatly desired, but it also gave me a fresh shot at a new social scene. Through the loudness of wall-shaking music and in the flicker of strobe lights, my girls introduced me to weekend nights full of themed dance parties, booty-shakin' hoochie attire, upside down margarita shots, and more-than-flirtatious fraternity boys.

In spinning party rooms on spinning dance floors with spinning friends, my hurt and insecurity fuzzed and swirled out of my mind. In this state, my past was of little concern to anyone, especially me. None of my teammates or any of the other students cared about who was crowned homecoming queen in high school or that I had been suspended for hitting Tyler. They didn't dislike me because of the cars my family owned or the vacations we took. No one made fun of my long hair, or my smile, or my clothes, or my basketball skills. They simply accepted me, and I finally belonged again. Yet, while I valued the inclusion that I found among my team and student body, I recognized that the threat of relational aggression would always loom nearby.

The vulnerability that came with peer incorporation became apparent when I noticed a love-triangle conflict between three of my team's veteran players. Even though their issues had resulted outside of basketball, their tension remained obvious during pre-season practices. Whenever all three girls were playing on the same team, two of them wouldn't pass the ball to the other; in-fact they acted as if she were invisible. My other teammates and coaches noticed and talked about this, but no one ever confronted the situation. I don't believe that any of us knew how to deal with it.

For once, I was relieved that I wasn't directly involved, but when one of the girls in the triangle approached me to take sides, I saw how easily it was to get sucked back in to relational aggression, and I wanted nothing to do with that familiar drama. It was intimidating to think that I could end-up in a comparable predicament if I defied the girls' power or denied them power in any way.

I was aware that a similar scenario could also develop with my roommates, but because I had not yet come across any signs of hostility or disagreement, I wasn't as worried. It seemed that if relational aggression were to occur, it would first happen among my teammates, where there was an internal challenge to be one of five starting players, to be that point-leader, record-breaker, and fan and media favorite.

Throughout my sports career, I had seen what happened when certain girls didn't get as much playing time or publicity as they felt they deserved. Instead of discussing their issues with the coaches or media representatives, they would take it out on whoever was getting more minutes or newspaper pictures and quotes, and, as a result, dissention occurred among players.

Sports were where competition among opponents *and* teammates was expected and evident. It was the type of contest that could bring me not only the success I had already treasured but the loss that I never again wanted. The memories of being bullied on my high school basketball team began leaking into my college team. I couldn't take another year of such aggression. Only months into the restored me, two weeks into the season, and after several days of serious consideration, I decided to withdraw from distinction by giving up the game I had spent half my life playing.

The night before I was to meet with my coaches, I stayed awake until daybreak, convincing myself that what I was preparing to do was necessary. A portion of me thought it was foolish to throw away the type of exposure that could totally rebuild my confidence and reputation, but no amount of press or social recognition could alleviate the suffering that I feared would once again be caused by relational aggression.

That afternoon, I quit basketball, and instantaneously my anger with the Honeybees resurfaced. I assumed that once my high school teammates and the Honeybees heard that I wasn't playing college ball any longer, they would attribute my quitting to the failure of my athletic or academic ability, not to the effect of what they had put me through. I wished to let my former teammates and the Honeybees know that I hadn't quit because I couldn't handle transitioning to college. I blamed those girls for every bad thing that had happened since my senior year of high school. It was because of them that I had been so fearful of having roommates and that I had to stop playing hoops. If it weren't for the girls' bullying, I would still be the vibrant, composed, normal person who I used to be, and I wouldn't be turning away from the things that I loved. I was convinced that the Honeybees had changed my life into something it wasn't supposed to be.

However, it was because my life hadn't turned out the way I envisioned it that I was motivated to convert my acrimony into inspiration. Never again wanting to be terrorized and sequestered by the events of my past, I set out to find a more effective, assuring, and lasting solution to defeating relational aggression, a remedy that wouldn't be found through the roar of a crazed crowd of basketball fans, in the packed bedrooms and basements of fraternity houses, or at the bottom of liquor bottles.

Hard Lessons

An entire year later, during the fall of my sophomore year, I finally realized that what I was looking for had always been right in front of me. I didn't discover this until one day at a campus Fellowship of Christian Athletes (FCA) meeting. FCA didn't usually create much hype, but on this day *everyone* was talking. I had participated in this particular club since I had quit basketball, and every week I listened to former athletes and area ministers deliver the same exhausted messages:

"Don't give in to peer pressure."
"Don't party."
"Don't drink."
"Don't have premarital sex."
"Dedicate yourselves to religion more than you do sports."

Just when I was starting to get jaded of hearing the same dry, repetitive lessons, I was roused by the testimony and teaching of Russ Clear, a member of a nationally recognized strength and power-lifting ministry known as "The Power Team."

On the afternoon Russ was to speak, I entered the FCA meeting room immediately sensing something out of the ordinary. The room usually buzzed with chatter, but today the members remained as hushed and still as deer being hunted during gun season. Those that dared to move slightly turned their heads and cautiously peered out the corners of their eyes to the far end of the room as if to send me a warning. Following their line of vision, I saw Russ for the first time, and I finally understood the reason for the unusual reactions. Fearing pulverization, I quickly found a seat and assumed the same please-don't-hurt-me disposition as everyone else.

Talk around campus was true. Russ was no joke. He *was* that hulk-like phenomenon that everyone proclaimed him to be. His 6'3," 310-pound stature, strict expression, shaved head, and 22.5-inch biceps promoted an image like that of a heavy-metal-head-banging-iron-pumping drill sergeant. Surely this wasn't a man who had come to speak about something as pure as God.

I thought about tiptoeing out of the meeting so I could mingle in the student center. It was Friday. I was done with a brain-straining week of classes. It was time for my fun to begin. *Whose frickin' idea was it to invite this whip-crackin' radical?* I thought. I definitely didn't feel like kickin' off my weekend dealing with this dude's sternness, but my leaving wasn't an option. There was something linking me to Russ that I just couldn't walk away from.

After the meeting began and Russ opened his discussion, my interpretation of him transformed. Russ wasn't some dictator with a halo, as I had previously thought. He was a selfless, peaceful, and captivating man. Underneath his striking burliness were ardent emotional and extraordinary, life-changing stories.

Russ had more baggage than anyone I knew, and as I heard about more and more of his dilemmas, the problems of my past seemed more than petty. Russ was a former Hell's Angel and Aryan brother who had spent most of his life in some of America's roughest prisons. He had recovered from mental and sexual abuse as a child, suicide attempts, gunshot wounds, and an addiction to crystal meth. His turn-around was enough to give any listener the motivation and hope to rise out of complication.

As he moved toward the end of his talk by speaking of how Christ gave up everything, even the love of God, to die for everyone's mistakes, his tone transitioned back to a seriousness that made my stomach flutter.

To accompany his message, he had brought along a two-by-four and a five-gallon bucket filled halfway with nails. Shifting into some kind of presentation, he pulled out a nail then picked up the board. He placed his left hand on the top end of the wood and pressed it down on the table so the board stood vertically. In his right hand he positioned a nail between his middle and ring fingers, sharp end pointed out. Making a fist, he—BAM—drove the nail through with a single punch. A wave of jerks, jolts, and jumps passed through the room. The board dropped, reverberating and shaking as if it had actually felt the blast. He grabbed another nail and—BAM—repeated the act once more. Picking up a third nail, he gathered an immense amount of force for what appeared was going to be the blow of all blows, but his fist stopped an inch shy of the board. Silently, he looked up at me then lowered his head and cried. I stared, startled and stupefied.

Using the wood as a symbol of the Cross, Russ had punched the nails through to display the brutal result of human imperfection and the precious gift that was produced in turn. His demonstration displayed a level of understanding and a depth of gratitude that I desired to have myself but hadn't yet grasped.

Still teary-eyed, Russ circled the room, carrying the bucket. He approached each person to ask if he or she would accept Christ's crucifixion and acknowledge

Him as the Savior. Everyone who agreed took their nail to a makeshift altar, the windowsill, to pray.

Even though I had already been asked this question and had already committed to it, I said yes. I had heard Christ's story numerous times, but on this occasion it shocked me, because it was presented in a way I had never before seen or felt.

Russ hadn't come to recite verbatim from a tattered, musty, prehistoric book. He brought a personal, refreshing spirituality that showed Jesus wasn't just a charm on a necklace, a figure on a stained glass window, or a lecture given from a pulpit on a routine Sunday morning. Russ represented Christ's realness and transformed my view of what it meant to be a Christian. With his nails and wood, he embedded Jesus within me like no one ever had.

In the room of the meeting, standing at the windowsill, I looked down to the parking lot. Sunshine glared off the tops of cars, but a dark gray weather front would soon bring rain to campus. My own emotional weathervane spun out of control. My mind was in a whirlwind, unsure of where to begin praying. *Why would anyone die for messed-up me?* I wondered. *I didn't deserve to have anyone "save my soul."*

A shadow crept over the windowsill and up my chest and face. A rumbling brewed within. I held my breath to avert weeping, and when I could no longer control my whimpers and sniffles, I erupted and scurried out of the room.

The revelation of Jesus' liveliness and my deadness hit me full-force, draining me of strength to function properly. Plagued by what I thought was my corroded character (an idea influenced by my being bullied), I bent over a wastebasket for a few minutes, gagging. My knees were so jiggly that I flopped down onto my right thigh. If Maria hadn't met up with me after the meeting, it would have taken me hours to make the two-block trek back to our room. She helped me up, locked her arm under mine, and upheld me as we walked.

I spent the rest of the afternoon in our suite's social room, zoned-out on our cheap, Wal-Mart futon. It usually bothered me to sit there because its mattress was so thin that its frame poked through, but this time I didn't even notice. I was only aware of the emotion that had been caused by Russ's words and actions.

For so long, I had thought that no one could understand me, that no one had gone through what I had. However, in considering what Jesus had done for me, I related my victimization to His and found there was at least one person who knew just as well as I did, only more, how it felt to go from being admired to being outcast.

Bad-mouthed, betrayed by friends, called names, laughed at, and shunned, (not to mention beaten, tortured, bloodied, stabbed, and killed), Jesus not only lived my experience, He dealt with all of the aggression that I never would have been able to take.[99] No one's story, not even Russ' story, had *ever* reduced the significance of my problems and experiences as much as Jesus' story.

I closed my eyes and replayed the picture and sound of Russ driving the nails through the board. As the scene repeated over and over in my mind, it evolved into vivid pieces of the Crucifixion.

A twinge traveled down my arm to my wrist. Christ's wrist. Flexing the tendons, I scrunched my face as I heard the pop of His punctured flesh. I felt the sting that the sharp, rusted iron sent screaming through His arteries and veins. I cringed at the widening of His incisions as the nails ripped through His nerves. The same heaviness that pulled Him downward on the Cross compacted me into a ball of remorse on the futon.

Intimately in tune to His wounds, I was disgusted that I was filled with such destructive, lethal hate. While I had wished fatal car accidents and life-threatening diseases upon my offenders, Jesus, who had been bullied to the most horrific extent, prayed that His abusers would be forgiven.[100] He was too good—more than too good—and I was just the opposite. In comparing all of the mistakes and retaliations I had made as a victim, to the purity and goodness He showed as a victim, I determined that I deserved His death much more, and I would have given my life to have been the substitute for those nails and His pain.

I wasn't meant to endure what Christ had gone through, though. No one was. He was specifically designed to be my replacement, to submit to the harshest penalty so I didn't have to.[101] More than ever, I was moved and impressed by the plan of His life and death.

Before, I thought that the only way I could earn back the value and success that had been taken away from me was to continually relive my past so that when relational aggression happened again I would know how to dodge it. However, dwelling on circumstances that couldn't be altered only deprived me of the goodness I was meant to find in Christ for the rest of my life.[102]

When I saw and felt Christ posted to the Cross, I was lifted out of my unproductiveness, recognizing that what had been taken away from me held no significance compared to the worth and victory that I was meant to have through the Lord. He died so I could escape my fears about relational bullying, and so I could be purified from my ugly reactions to it.[103] Even though I had this breakthrough, it would take several more hard lessons to ditch my self-reliance and trust God entirely.

The following evening, I learned the first of those lessons. After Maria and I debated how to kill boredom in our rural, every-business-closes-after-supper college town, we settled on a Sigma Chi dance party. We needed to loosen-up before heading out, so we each downed a bottle of Mad Dog 20/20 and a couple of Jack Daniel's cocktails then staggered out the door to tally-up another party-girl weekend.

The next morning, I groaned into consciousness. Waking with a blank memory, a sore butt, and a churning stomach, I was unable to rush down my loft ladder to the bathroom before I splattered my bedding with putrid regret. This was the first time I had ever vomited from drinking. For the past year and a half, I had been proud to have said I always defeated "the heave" and only woke with a headache, but, on this day, as I heaved … and heaved … and heaved, all my pride left me, and I was taken back to the nails and the board, to the Crucifix and His wounds.

Through alcohol, I was reminded of how there was no coping mechanism but God that could help me get past my past. I had no influence over an outcome and a future that had already been determined. Once again, I was plagued with guilt, knowing that drinking myself to oblivion and sickness was unappreciative toward everything I had felt after FCA. The feeling delivered through Russ's talk was too strong to drink away and forget about. It had been sent to invoke a change within me that called me to acknowledge that the stronger solution I had been looking for was *Jesus*. He was that lasting and assuring remedy that could bring me the peace and acceptance that I wanted, and now it was time to surrender to Him.

For the remainder of the day, I stared at the bottom of a wet, spew-soaked trash bag, pleading for God's forgiveness, and in my distress, I finally let Him relieve my desperation.

Turbulence

My stomach and liver didn't function properly for the next three days, but at least my brain was quicker to jump back on the path of production. My potentially fatal error hadn't instantly converted me into a brand-spankin'-new person, but it had coerced me to return to my Bible.

Other than in Sunday school, I had never read the Bible on a regular basis. I had tried, but I always became impatient and discouraged by its tiring lists of Old Testament names. As a result, I simply gave up, and, from then until now, I completely discounted the Bible as a source of comfort and assistance. Plunging back into its pages, I was not only awakened to its guidance and support, I was linked to its characters through what I thought was only a contemporary problem.

While the people of the Bible weren't familiar with the term "relational bullying," they were definitely involved with it. For example, in Genesis 37, Joseph's eleven brothers schemed against him, abandoned him, and sold him into slavery in order to eliminate him from future success.[104] In Numbers 12, Moses' siblings, Miriam and Aaron, badmouthed him when they became envious of his authority.[105] Judges 16 shows how Samson's lover, Delilah, backstabbed and betrayed him to his enemies, the Philistines.[106] First Samuel 18–31 tells of years of harassment that ensued when King Saul couldn't tame his hostility and resentment toward David.[107] In the book of Nehemiah, Sanballat, Tobiah, and Geshem attempted to destroy Nehemiah's hard work and reputation, as they mocked, insulted, plotted against him, and manipulated their friends to do the same. The men even sent him hate mail.[108] In the New Testament, Acts 6–7, Stephen's peers, angered and intimidated by his conviction, secretly convinced others to lie about him and call him names.[109] Plus, there were a number of times in the book of Acts when large groups of people became abusive toward Paul. Often, alliances of conspirators formed against him, intending to eliminate him as a threat to their power.[110]

Although thousands of years separated me from these characters, our experiences converged. Their stories gave me a further sense of placement and led me to analyze what they had done and what I could do to defeat such bullying situations. Thankfully, sure-fire solutions lay within God's Word.

Verses like 1 Peter 5:7, which said, "Cast all your anxiety on him because he cares for you," made me realize that I needed to stop stressing about being re-ruined by relational aggression. If it came about, Psalm 110:1, Zephaniah 3:19, and Romans 12:19 guaranteed that God would handle bullies so I wouldn't have to.

> Sit at my right hand until I make your enemies a footstool for your feet. (Psalm 110:1)

> At that time I will deal with all who oppressed you. (Zephaniah 3:19)

> Do not take revenge, my friends, but leave room for God's wrath, for it is written: "It is mine to avenge; I will repay," says the Lord. (Romans 12:19)

There were several verses like Luke 6: 27–36 that said all I had to do was to con-trol myself from mental, verbal, and physical retaliation, and instead I had to live in peace with my offenders, encourage them, and love and respect them.[111]

> But I tell you who hear me: Love your enemies, do good to those who hate you, bless those who curse you, pray for those who mistreat you. If someone strikes you on one cheek, turn to him the other also. If someone takes your cloak, do not stop him from taking your tunic. Give to everyone who asks you, and if anyone takes what belongs to you, do not demand it back. Do to others as you would have them do to you.

> If you love those who love you, what credit is that to you? Even 'sinners' love those who love them. And if you do good to those who are good to you, what credit is that to you? Even 'sinners' do that. And if you lend to those from whom you expect repayment, what credit is that to you? Even 'sinners' lend to 'sinners,' expecting to be repaid in full. But love your enemies, do good to them, and lend to them without expecting to get anything back. Then your reward will be great, and you will be sons [and daughters] of the Most High, because he is kind to the ungrateful and wicked. Be merciful, just as your Father is merciful. (Luke 6:27–36)

Well, that was easier said than done. God's instructions were the most simplis-tic directions I could have received, but my emotions didn't want to cooperate in acting upon the instructions. Yet, I knew in my heart that I had to start taking action. Feeling as if it were vital to meet these principles, I joined another well-known campus Christian club, The Rock, hoping to find the accountability and support that would rally me to live up to God's standards.

Since my freshman year, I had been skeptical of this campus fellowship group. Talk around school was that the students involved were a clique of lame, holier-than-thou, virgin Bible-bangers that spent their weekends locked in their rooms studying.

Because I had listened to the rumors, I was worried that participating in The Rock meant that both my secular and non-secular communities might outcast me. I could be rejected by mainstream campus if I was seen as a "dorky do-no-wrong," and I could be rejected by the dorky do-no-wrongs if I didn't live a virtuous enough lifestyle. In high school, there were many times that I wished my peers wouldn't have judged me using other peoples' negative opinions, and now, as a sophomore in college, although I still listened and considered hearsay, I finally understood the importance of dismissing rumors. I needed to experience The Rock and its members for myself, and if in that process I had to sacrifice belonging and risk denunciation in order to grow my faith, I was willing to take that chance.

Upon entering the room where my first meeting was held, I felt as if rejection would be a likely outcome. An obvious disparity among the attendees left me outnumbered by my own gender. My temperature rose as a group of about five girls examined and approached me. Fortunately, I encountered a contrasting image to that which had been rumored, and I couldn't resist but to return their welcoming smiles and handshakes.

It didn't take but a couple of meetings before the kindness of several young women moved me out of my reservations and nearer to the support for which I was searching. Soon, my schedule was loaded with lunch and dinner dates, movie nights, and other get-togethers, and with stabilized security, my confidence climbed. Yet, while I gained new girl friends, old friendships began fading away.

Whenever I returned from fellowship, I was quick to share my excitement with Liz, Katie, and Maria. They were all Christians, and I thought they would appreciate any upbeat news I could bring back. However, the more enthusiasm I displayed, the less attention I received from them.[112]

This first became obvious at the beginning of spring semester, immediately after we returned from our nearly month-long Christmas break. That was when Liz, Katie, and Maria suddenly stopped speaking to me. Loss of contact with Maria, unfortunately, but understandably, happened during Christmas break, when she decided to leave school and pursue endeavors elsewhere. Still, there seemed to be no reason for Liz and Katie's aloofness.

At first, I took their behavior to be bad-day blues, or I bet they were just trying to get through another gloomy, depressing Ohio winter. However, this didn't make sense, because, only days after we returned from break, I overheard them cheerfully and laughingly talking to each other and other people.

As weeks went by and their silence toward me remained, I tried not to overreact or take their manners personally, but apprehension began to consume me. Normally, because of our closeness and the candidness of our discussions, I knew nearly everything that was going on in their lives. Now, I was a clueless outsider, and I couldn't think of much that I had done to cause the distancing.

Maybe Liz and Katie were acting this way because they felt as if they were losing me to my new friends of The Rock. Taking this into consideration, I made sure to give my roommates more of my attention by making out-of-my-way efforts to communicate.

Whenever they were in our common room or the bathroom, I would purposely enter just to talk. I would "coincidentally" walk out the door with them when they left for class, and I would even time-it-out to meet them as they came out of their academic buildings. "What've you been up to? How's your day? Whatcha doin' this weekend?" I would inquire. I even tried to persuade them to attend The Rock with me. Attempt after attempt, I asked the same old questions and got the same cold, minimal responses until eventually I ran out of ways to generate dialogue.

As badly as I wanted to eliminate the tension, I backed off rather than simply asking the girls what was bothering them. In doing so, I hoped that I would give Liz and Katie the cooperation and care that they needed in order to work through whatever they were coping with. Though the longer I bit my tongue, stayed quiet, and left them alone, the more they disengaged. They were always too busy to meet for meals, their weekends were always occupied with other people, and their bedroom door was always closed.

Maybe my roommates and their door would open back up after their tennis season was over. I had frequently heard from the two of them about the conflicts that occurred among their teammates. Perhaps they had become consumed in the stress of a dispute. They probably just needed time and space to get through. Yet, when their season ended, their attitudes didn't change, and I became increasingly upset and insulted.

The excuses I created for Liz and Katie's behavior never ceased to fail. One afternoon I entered their room intending to socialize. They weren't there, but it was the absence of something else that troubled me. All the photographs featuring us had been taken down and replaced with new pictures of people I didn't know. At first, I rationalized a redecoration in progress, but when I peeked into their room a few times after, I saw that the snapshots remained missing.

My seeing them around campus made me feel even worse. Whenever I encountered them in the fitness center, bookstore, or dining halls, they pretended not to notice me by turning their focus to someone or something else. More slighting was when I came across them on the walkways. They would quicken their pace or take a shortcut in the opposite direction.

Several years prior, I wouldn't have hesitated to ask the reason for being snubbed. However, now I wasn't as forthcoming, because the only way to find out if Liz and Katie were unhappy was to confront them, and if I did, I might feel the same damaging hurt that had wrecked me before. Provoking unnecessary drama was not what I wanted. The easier and less painful option was to anticipate that the predicament would resolve over time. Yet, suppressing the problem and hoping it would just go away landed me in my first socially altering collegiate conflict.

Before Christmas break, my roommates and I had agreed to live together during the following academic year. Now that it was spring semester, and we would no longer have Maria as a roommate, Liz, Katie, and I immediately looked for a replacement for next year. If we could find a fourth roommate, we wouldn't risk being separated and assigned random dorms and roommates. Because Maria and I had again planned to share a bedroom, I felt a large responsibility in finding someone to take her place, and I did shortly after. Yet, had I known the detriment that was about to occur between Liz, Katie, and me, I might have reconsidered my choice in future roommates.

It had been over a month since Liz, Katie, and I reworked our plan. I believed our decision was final, but I was wrong. One evening, when I was hanging out in the hallway of my dorm, I was informed by my friend, Beth, that Liz and Katie were committed to other housing arrangements because they didn't want to room with Bri, the girl I had lined up to fill Maria's vacancy.

Beth's sorry-I-had-to-tell-you expression unintentionally flattened me. As she repeated the details of our conversation, my throat swelled. I took two hard swallows but that queasy crying feeling only grew.

NO WAY am I being ditched! I was suspicious. *Beth has to be stirring trouble*, I thought. *Yeah, that's it. She's one of those girls that just can't stand to see things work out for other girls.* If Beth were the envious, vindictive type, it would have brought me a lot of relief, and I wouldn't have to worry about being back-doored by my best friends or making unexpected and frantic changes to my housing paperwork, which was due the *very* next day. However, that just wasn't Beth. She was honest and wholesome, and her story explained why Liz and Katie hadn't been acknowledging me.

Even through all of my roommates' strange behaviors, I never considered our future living arrangement to be the problem, and therefore I never thought to verify our rooming deal. When, and even after I told them about locating a new roommate, they never acted bothered or said, "No, that won't work. We have to find someone else." So, I believed Bri would be a suitable replacement. Surely, if Liz and Katie were uncomfortable, they would have told me so we could work to improve the matter. As dearest friends, we talked about *everything* ... except this.

Unlike the reaction I had had to Tyler's rumor in high school, I stood around and thought about what Beth had told me. While my mind skimmed through all of the fun times I had had with my roommates, my regret shifted into anger. *How could they not have felt close enough to me to approach me with this? Did they* really *think that if they didn't tell me it wouldn't hurt me? Did they* really *think that if they gradually distanced themselves from me, life between us would go on as normal?* Then again, I had.

If *only* I would have forced myself to talk to them weeks ago. If *only* I would have simply asked why they were behaving differently, we might have been able to avoid this mess. Even if we had to part as roommates we could have remained friends, and I could have secured a different housing position, but now there was no time to dream-up "what might have been's," and there was no time to wait for my emotions to settle either.

Unwillingly, I entered Liz and Katie's room to confirm and confront the issue. Liz lay motionless on her top bunk, either asleep or reluctant to talk, and Katie shrugged her shoulders, unemotionally responding, "We thought you made other plans."

I blew, raving about their coldness toward me. With rage, I exited, slamming the door that adjoined our rooms, shutting out some of the only people that I had felt safe among since my senior year of high school.[113] Once again, I was shattered.

For the remainder of the spring semester, the activity within our room was quite silent. It was outside our walls that noise was made. It was apparent that Liz and Katie had influenced our friends' perceptions. Girls who we had hung out with on the weekends and ate meals with throughout the week quickly dropped me and came off as if they were "too good" to associate with me. More devastating was learning of the same reaction from Maria.

After I came back to school from a weekend at home, my floormate and friend, Sondra, told me that Maria had been back to visit Liz and Katie. Sondra didn't exactly know what had happened between my roommates and me. Naturally, she was confused when she ran into them and asked where I was and why I wasn't with them, and Maria responded with an eye-roll and a huff, sardonically clarifying that she *definitely* hadn't come back to see me.

Maria and I had been closest out of my roommates. It had been disappointing when she left school, and we fell out of contact, but I just thought she had stopped replying to my e-mails and phone calls because she was busy with new undertakings, not because our relationship had become a conflict of interest.

My roommates' and their friends' actions were subtler than those of the Honeybees. Nonetheless, I was left with that unwanted, demeaning, ganged-up-on feeling. After everything I had went through in high school, I couldn't believe I had been so foolish to think that I could regain authentic, lasting friendship in college. Girls just weren't dependable, and the only way I knew how to deal with girls who hurt me was to cast a few dirty looks their way then ignore them as if we had never been friends. Thus, I completely disregarded Liz, Katie, and their friends for the rest of the school year.

This relapse was enough to send me dive-bombing into self-pity and blame, but I refused to crash into that all-too familiar, grounding depression. Instead, I stepped on my emotional brake, leveled my movement, gripped tight my controls, and braced through the turbulence by seeking recovery in God.

A Visitor's Grasp

Just days after my fallout with Liz and Katie, I immersed myself in the company of my fellow female club members of The Rock. Meeting after meeting, I had witnessed them embrace each other's difficulties. Now, it was my turn to bring my distresses to them.

Confiding in my new girlfriends deepened my bond with them. Still, memories of deceit left me feeling as if I would never be totally fulfilled by human connection. What I wanted was what no person could give. I wanted just one, consistently encouraging and forgiving relationship that was guaranteed to uphold when the rest failed. The perfect relationship that I wanted was what *only* the Lord could provide.

God had never acted the same way my antagonists had. He had never spread His aggression to others. He had never whispered bad things about me to His friends or called me hurtful names. He had never "accidentally" bumped into me while walking to class, and He had never excluded me from girls' night out. God had never been my bully. It was *people* who had done those things, and if relational aggression were to hurt me again, it would result from the choices and imperfections of *people*.

Never would God produce the same result. Only He had brought me out of misery. Only He offered the unswerving security I searched for.

> "For I know the plans I have for you," declares the Lord, "plans to prosper you and not harm you, plans to give you hope and a future." (Jeremiah 29:11)

God would never abandon me.[114] Only He held true to the promises that everyone else had broken. He held every feature that I had failed to obtain from people. Only He could be my number-one companion, because it was only He who could fulfill my every need, and it was time that I stopped focusing on how badly people had and could hurt me and start focusing on how greatly God loved me. Once I committed all of my attention to His capabilities, I no longer feared being attacked.

It was during an evening of fellowship, amid the flicker of candlelight and soothing strums of acoustic guitars, that I set aside my anxiety of being bullied and joined in and belted out some of my favorite praise songs—"Open the Eyes of My Heart," "God of Wonders," and "Did You Feel the Mountains Tremble." That night, in a room full of people who seemed to have suddenly discovered their vocal cords, my only absorption was uniting with my peers, especially my girlfriends, to exalt God.

When fellowship concluded, I was one of the last to exit. I bounced out the door giddily conversing with a group of about six girls. I couldn't believe that I already felt at-home with them. A portion of me couldn't hack girls, but more of me couldn't help but to gravitate toward them.

When I departed from them and returned to my dark room, there was no way I could start any homework. Still jacked-up, I exuberantly paced and jumped around my tiny cubicle. After several song-and-dance outbursts, the moon's illumination called upon me, and I became settled enough to squat beneath my window and pray.

Nearing an hour of rambling, doubting whether I was making much sense, I finally flipped on my light and sat down at my desk to read a chapter of E.M. Forester's *Howard's End*. Fifteen minutes and only a few paragraphs later, I tossed the book on the floor and tried to occupy myself in other ways.

I checked my e-mail—nothing but spam. I opened my fridge—nothing but garbage-bound leftovers. I turned on my television—nothing but reruns. The screen sucked away an episode of *Everybody Loves Raymond,* and I plopped down in my Lazyboy. I couldn't lean back to relax, though. I stayed on the edge of my chair, craving God.

I closed my eyes and again thanked Him for keeping at me through all of the times that I had insisted He leave me alone, but my words just weren't enough. I needed to convey and *feel* a more expressive message.

I already knew the profundity of Christ's Crucifixion. I had been there. Been Him. Been bitten by the chill of wind and sin. I had felt His punctures. I had seen His wounds stretch and ooze. It was my futon meditation that impacted me like nothing before. I *had* to revisit that day. This time I backtracked, inviting the intensity of His soul-crushing walk to Golgotha.

◆   ◆   ◆

Pelted by pebbles. Stung by stones. He tripped and tottered His way down a road thriving with deadness. Few mourned. Many cheered. Skulking, snarling soldiers and spectators savored in His subjugation. They jabbed and clawed at His splintered, sliced, gashed tissue. Spit, sweat, dirt, and blood blurred and burned His vision.

Thousands empowered against *one* debilitated man.

I felt for Him in a way I had never felt for anyone. Sidelined, I would not amplify His agony. I fought the flow, faltering within the mass.

He passed. He stumbled.

Synchronously, we collapsed into a footpath of fury. His maimed body sandwiched between the timber and earth. Both of our bodies smothered by heaviness, crushed between lasting life and perdition.

Struggling to His feet, He dragged on, but I could not withstand. Bopped and bumped by the mob, I crawled to His tracks, sweeping through His trail of blood speckle and streak, where hope soaked the sands of adversity.

◆   ◆   ◆

Alone in my room I heard no sound. No shoe brushed the carpet. No mouth made noise. I had already closed and locked my door, but indeed, I had a visitor whose presence put me totally at ease.

On the edge of my chair, I lifted my once dirt-dusted, ruby-stained hands. My guest approached—*Closer*—Tears tickled the curves of my nose and lips—*Closer*—Goosebumps sprouted over my extremities—*Closer*—Wrapped up in security, saturated with more calmness and bliss than ever, the hands of the Holy Spirit grasped and squeezed my palms, giving me the hope to survive every relationship to come.[115]

I Hate Girls: The Sequel

Unfortunately, a social breakdown followed my spiritual breakthrough. My junior year would be my most challenging year yet. That fall semester was when I wore off the letters on my laptop's keys, sped through cases of ink cartridges and a forest of printing paper, and took up secondary residency in the library—all unlike my roommate, Bri.

After Liz and Katie had forced Bri and I to change our housing plan, we frantically searched for two more roommates to fill a quad, which I found in my Geology classmate, Meghan, and her sorority sister, Stephanie. The four of us ended up having to live in the oldest, stalest dorm on campus, but the bonus to having hammer-banging pipes and ghostly-creaking floors was that we got a larger-than-average corner room, which included a private bath (a must-have for girls). In my dilapidated dorm, I would start anew in the company of entirely different roommates.

Yeah right. Bri and I didn't exactly mesh with Meg and Steph's already established Greek group, where friends, flings, and fun seemed to come at a cost. Unless we pledged, Bri and I felt as if we would never totally be "in" with Meg, Steph, and company. Bri and I would never totally be "in" with each other either.

Bri was a natural smarty-pants, a moody, West-Coast daddy's girl who had spent a portion of her high school career in therapy for difficulty with relationships. I never probed for specific or elaborate reasons as to why she went through treatment, but I empathized, feeling relational bullying must have been the culprit. Only, I was too optimistic to see that we might have been on different ends of the same issue. We were on different ends of basically everything.

While I arranged my schedule so that I could get classes out of the way in the morning, Bri refused to wake up before noon. I spent my day happily hanging out with my boyfriend, working out, and studying. In contrast, Bri spent much of her day munching on entire boxes of Cap'n Crunch and Life while lounging in front of game shows and soap operas, that is, when she wasn't on the phone yelling at and crying to her long-distant boyfriend.

It didn't take me long to figure out why the plans for my previous rooming arrangement hadn't worked out. Liz's cousin, who also attended our college, had roomed with Bri the year before, and it was obvious that through the connection, Liz and Katie had uncovered something they didn't like about Bri. It would have been nice to at least get a warning from Liz and Katie, because clearly I didn't know what I was getting myself into with Bri.

In the beginning, Bri wasn't *that* bad. We had a lot of hyped-up-on-caffeine, goofball moments, and we both loved the vibes and strums of The Dave Matthews Band. I considered her a friend. Unlike Liz and Katie, Bri hadn't walked out on our plan. I was grateful to her for that, and whenever I got annoyed with her, I remembered this. I also remembered that in less than one year, I would be livin' it up in a senior single. Having roommates didn't necessarily bother me any longer, but not having roommates excited me. In the privacy of my own room, I wouldn't have to worry about constantly adjusting my personality or schedule to meet my roommate's needs. Yet, of course, a squeaky-clean transition into my own dorm room wouldn't be possible, because I couldn't escape another academic year without one more roommates-gone-bad story.

The problems between Bri and me began only two months after we had moved in together. In mid-October, Bri found out that her mom had been diagnosed with the early stages of Alzheimer's disease. Because Bri's family lived over 2,000 miles away, I could only image how difficult it was for her to deal with such devastating news. It was one of those helpless situations where I longed to take some kind of action, but at the same time, I felt as if there was nothing I could do to make things better. I sensitively offered my condolences, assuming that Bri knew she could vent freely to me about her mom's deterioration.

Weeks went by, and Bri talked to me about her mom only once. She went about her routine and appeared to be holding strong, but she was actually harboring more stress than she let on, and she was about to detonate.

It happened one evening when, for once, we were both at our desks studying. I was stressing over how to translate attorney case-brief jargon about student regulation in the eighth circuit court of appeals into 20-pages of term paper readability, while Bri was fussing about her "massive" workload—what I considered a tiny, six to eight page sociology paper. Less than an hour into our work, Bri sighed, raised her arms, and leaned back in her chair to stretch. Unsurprisingly, she wasn't into pulling an all-nighter, or even a half-nighter, or a quarter-nighter.

It was about that time again—T.V. time. Away went the books, out came the cereal, and unexpectedly, in walked two of Bri's gal-pals, Tiffany and Julie, I assumed because their own television had been broken. *Social time while I'm straining my brain?* *Yep*, I thought, remembering that compromise was a huge part of having roommates. I zipped up my shut-it-all-out, thinking tent and pressed on.

Half-an-hour later, when the mix of three giddy girls and a blaring television was no longer tolerable, I put on my headphones and listened to music, hoping one consistent noise would drown-out all other sounds. When that didn't work I asked if Tiffany and Julie's television was fixed, thinking they might consider relocating.

"NO," Tiffany sharply retorted.

"Oo-kay ...," I replied as I turned back around to refocus, taken aback and feeling as if Tiffany's response was a bit overdramatic.

Only seconds later, when the blinking cursor on my computer screen hypnotized me, and the tunes that streamed into my ears continued to keep me sidetracked, our heavy birch door slammed with such force I almost gave myself whiplash. The girls had turned off the television. Our room was empty. "Ooo-kkk-aa-yyy? That's odd," I said. "They seriously can't be mad about *that* ... can they?" I opened the door to catch them in the hallway, but they had left too fast. It was possible that now *I* was the one overreacting (that's typical of females, *right?*). Maybe something big and urgent swept them off like a PMS craving for a chocolate-M&M-Oreo-hot fudge sundae. I glanced at my purse, tempted to make my own ice cream run, but I resisted the urge and quickly got back to finishing my footnotes.

After I completed my paper about an hour later, I was in great need of a refreshing shower. As I made my way to the bathroom, a note that had been slid under the crack of my main door caught my attention. It was from Bri, and, as the note explained, the girls *had* left because they were angry.

All you EVER *do anymore is study and spend time with your boyfriend—you* NEVER *have time for me. You're No fun. You're mean. You're negative. And Tiffany and Julie see how rude you're being to me!* Also, Bri said I had ruined the new episode of *Friends*, thus ruining her entire evening (possibly her entire week). The three girls would be in Tiffany and Julie's room if I wanted to talk.

I had no idea Bri felt this way. I *had* been majorly zoned in on my schoolwork, and I hadn't been devoting much attention to anything or anyone else. Still, after reading her letter, I immediately felt attacked. It seemed that my stable, happy, romantic relationship and my consistent, devoted work ethic was what Bri held against me. This explanation might very well have supported Bri's behavior. According to feminist Phyllis Chesler, author of *Woman's Inhumanity to Woman*, it often occurs that when another girl or woman attempts to succeed at something, other females hold that against her.[116] However, I believe there was more to Bri's reaction than just envy. As I look back and consider her mother's illness, I now understand that Bri obviously wanted more emotional availability from me than I knew about and that I *couldn't* know about unless she communicated her needs to me. For all I knew, her mother's health was the same as it had been. If Bri would have said, "Hey, can I talk to you," or "Hey, ya wanna meet for dinner so we can catch up," I would have gladly set aside time to do so, but she didn't. Although Bri and I weren't best buds, I wasn't so insensitive or heartless that I couldn't provide emotional support for her. Lately, she had started spending so much time with Tiffany and Julie that I assumed she was getting the support she needed from them and didn't need as much from me.

Realizing that Bri had involved Tiffany and Julie in our conflict was what really popped my top. Bri, like many females (including myself), confided in her inner circle rather than tackling her issues head-on, and in doing so, she addressed her frustrations to everyone but me.[117]

Still standing by our door, holding the note, I feared that in a matter of minutes the majority of my dorm, possibly the whole university (there were only 1,800 students enrolled) would hear that I was a "study-crazy bitch." Panic came upon me. It was the same type of feeling I had experienced when Tyler spread the rumor about me in high school.

That's it. It was time to let Bri know how much I didn't appreciate her demonizing me and turning others against me.[118] Looking back, I wonder why I hadn't learned to control myself by now. My if-*that's*-what-you-think-of-me-then-I'll-really-show-you-my-nasty-side attitude took over. And there I went, stomping out the door, buying into and supporting exactly what had been said, blinded by the fact that a three-verses-one confrontation wasn't going to land me or the other girls anywhere but hurt.

Some of the very attributes that I considered to be my strengths were what the girls proceeded to shred to bits. I didn't even know Tiffany and Julie that well, but Bri had excessively and exaggeratedly familiarized them with comments that I didn't even know I had made. I felt discouraged and insulted. Bri hadn't got the nurturing that she wanted from me, so this trashing was my payback, and I had jumped right in and twist-tied myself up.[119]

Near the end of our confrontation, I stepped back into my "I hate girls" mode, telling the three of them, "*This* is why *I'm* not friends with girls like *y-o-o-o-u-u-u*"—and that shut them up. They looked at me shocked, like they were unaware that they had a specific categorization.

Yeah, girls like Y-O-U, I mentally repeated as I exited the argument, prideful that I had taken back what I thought was control but was really only an equally demeaning slam.

Later that night, I met with one of the residential supervisors, Diane, to discuss what had happened. Looking back, I wished that I would have spoken to a mediator before stepping into such a wounding quarrel. However, Bri had already met with Diane, and it was clear that I wouldn't be getting any I-feel-for-you points from her. I had been screwed-over by girls *again*.

Emerging from Diane's office, I returned to my room only to hear Tiffany filling Meg and Steph in on half-truths and all the bad things I had supposedly said about them. I asked Tiffany to leave and quickly tried to repair her lies. Meg and Steph assured me that they held no harsh feelings toward me, but I sensed that there was nothing I could do to repair what Tiffany had done.

I returned to my room to let my anger cool-off. After a few hours of settling down, the typical, feminine caretaker role within me kicked in, wanting to work things out. I hadn't liked the outcome among Liz, Katie, Maria, and me, and I didn't want it to be the same way with Bri, Tiffany, and Julie. I didn't necessarily want to associate with the girls any longer, but I wanted them to respect me and vice versa. Several days later, I asked Diane if she would mediate, but she told me that Bri had already said she wanted nothing to do with a resolution.

I was convinced the only thing Bri wanted was to cause me more aggravation. While she had agreed to move out, she did so at a painstakingly slow speed. It took her over a month to finally start packing her possessions. Everyday, I envisioned a redecoration of my soon-to-be-all-mine pad. Yet, it was as if Bri could hear the redesign go off in my brain. She would constantly change her mind about moving, telling our housing advisors that *she* shouldn't be the one who had to relocate, therefore giving me the headache of possibly having to live with her for the rest of the year.

Bri played as if she didn't want to move out, but in essence she already had. She had unofficially filled a vacancy in Tiffany and Julie's room, but she left most of her belongings in our room, untouched, to keep the tension active. She hardly ever came to our room. If she needed something, she sent her Pleaser/Wannabe/Messenger, Tiffany. I didn't run into Tiffany much, but I could always tell when she had stopped in because she would leave post-it note messages stuck on my desk and refrigerator that told me I was "immature" and that I needed to "grow up."

One evening, I ran into Tiffany at a local restaurant in which I was unaware she worked as a hostess. Several of her female co-workers were around when she cheerfully asked me how I had been and what I had been up to, as if we were so chummy or something. *What a convenient time for mind games*, I thought. I wasn't into playing or winning her I'm-gonna-make-you-look-bad-and-myself-look-like-a-saint competition, so I proceeded out the door without comment and without being seated for dinner.

The next day, Tiffany sent me an instant message that told me I had made a fool out of myself and her co-workers thought I had acted "stupid" and "child-ish." She even said that my boyfriend, who had been with me, thought that I was an idiot for not speaking to her. (When we were leaving, he had tried to get my attention (but couldn't) because he thought Tiffany was trying to tell me that I had left something behind in the lobby, and Tiffany thought he was trying to get me to talk to her). I deleted the message without reading its entirety. Because this wasn't the first menacing instant message that I had received, I blocked Tiffany's username. However, her harassments were only warm-ups for what I was about to experience from Bri.

Following an evening at the library, I returned to my room to a rare moment of Bri's presence. Even before our rumble, Bri hardly ever associated with Meg and Steph, but tonight she was in their room socializing. Lately, Bri and Meg had become quite chipper with each other. I had seen them walking to class together, which was way not normal, and I figured that their newly found closeness was a result of my inability to mend Bri and Tiffany's fabrications.

In Geology class, Meg no longer talked to me unless I spoke to her. She kept her responses super short and punctuated with eye-rolls. Although, I could never decipher her mean eye-rolls from her typical, sarcastic, "that's just Meg" eye-rolls. To me, any kind of eye-roll was still an eye-roll, and every time Meg responded to me in this way, I wondered why it seemed as if girls had to live for the "gasp and gossip," why they were so easily swayed by each other, and why they had to have a reason to hate and turn against each other—more specifically, to hate and turn against *me*.

When Bri heard me enter our room, she scampered over to our suite as if not wanting to be caught. We said "hi," to each other, and I asked if she would be sure to tell me when I had received important telephone messages or when a visitor came to see me.

A couple days before, one of my study partners had stopped by hoping to meet with me, but I wasn't present. He said he had left a message with Bri, but Bri failed to communicate it, which resulted in a bit of a scheduling jam for me. Before our conflict, Bri and I had always written each other's missed phone calls and visitors on our dry erase board. It wasn't like her not to. Unsure of whether she had failed to inform me out of spite or if she had forgot due to the amount of stress she was under, I simply asked if she would try to remember next time. I should have known not to start our dialogue with a confrontation. I might have been far more productive if I would have eased into the request, but I had already blown that chance, and my mistake caused Bri to do some blowing up of her own, just like I had done with my past roommates.

At the time, I saw no reason for my question to create a "fly off the handle" moment, but Bri turned it into just that. She had internalized so much frustration and anger toward me that she started yelling and frantically gathering clothes and books. She moved like a tornado, with her arms flailing in mad orchestra conductor style. I don't think she knew what she was grabbing, tossing, or flinging. There was no stopping or calming her.

I stood in the doorway of our bathroom, fascinated. *Why did it have to be like this?* I thought. *Why was it such a big deal for me to ask a question?* Wasn't communication the key to any relationship? Why was confrontation between girls such an off-limits, touchy thing? I felt as if there was hardly ever a sensible medium. It was just like a female to bury her conflicts, irritations, and hostilities until she either ignored the troublesome relationship right out of her life or she ended up exploding, just as I had before and just as Bri was about to do.[120]

In the midst of many of Bri's "You're so this," and, "You're so that" remarks, she reared back with mighty force, and flung the bathroom door shut, hitting the entire right side of my body. My fiery reflection melted the lacquer. I heard Bri grab a few more things then exit by slamming our main door (she really had a thing for slamming doors). True, I was tempted to chase her down and use my fist to put a dent in the back of her head, but, thankfully, the bathroom door served as a much-needed boundary, my signal to take a much-needed cool shower instead of resorting to violence again.

Later that evening, I caught Diane in the hallway, where she was obviously on her way to something much more important. Rather than filing a violence report or even asking if we could, at a later time, talk about what had happened between Bri and me, Diane cut me off and brusquely said, "Everything's being taken care of. Just sit tight until she finds another place to live." Diane left me standing in the hallway, feeling rejected and unimportant.

Had I just met the daughter of my high school administrator, Mr. Littlefield? "Move 'em out, get 'em through, and hope to God the next roommate has a higher tolerance level" seemed to be the general philosophy of the housing advisors, most of whom were primarily women. I knew of several girls who had been through numerous roommates. Whether they were difficult to live with I don't personally know, but the housing advisors just kept cranking girls through the system, abiding by some unwritten "When girls fight, we cover it up" policy.

Lost as to how to prevent or correct this reoccurring scenario, I re-entered counseling at the university's counseling center, but, after a month of sessions, my counselor couldn't even tell me that what I was experiencing was called relational aggression. She didn't understand, and it always ticked me off when another female didn't "get it." She just kept answering my questions with open-ended questions like, "Why do you think girls can be so mean?" or, "What do you think you can do about that?" I desperately wanted answers and direction from my counselor, but the only thing I received was further frustration.

My university's counselors and housing advisors claimed to see issues like mine over and over, but the only explanation anyone could come up with for the behavior was that it was a "girl thing," brought on by the girl who was doing the most "complaining." Diane and my counselor informed me that the tension between Bri and me had been caused by my directness, as if it was a bad thing to be straightforward. Diane told me that she couldn't really relate to someone like me, that she related more to Bri, because like Bri, she was also non-confrontational. Diane's statement baffled me. She didn't have to like confrontation—who does? Not me—but as someone responsible for managing hundreds of students, she was telling me she would rather not deal with a problem?!

Now, in hindsight, I think I understand Diane's stance. Generally, most people interpret directness from women as unnatural, difficult, mean, pushy, insensitive, uncompromising, out-of-control, or just plain bitchy.[121] I didn't agree with these labels. If anything, I felt as if I could have been more direct. All of us could have been more direct in many ways, especially by telling each other (in private) what was bothering us at the time we felt bothered. Then there wouldn't have been any of our "read between the lines" interpretations as to why we did the things that we did or said the things that we said. However, being straightforward was a scary thing, as it is for many females who don't want to take the chance of feeling let-down or being shamed by others.[122]

Thank God fall semester ended soon enough. For nearly all of spring semester, I kept the door closed to Meg and Steph's room, and I enjoyed not having roommates.

When my senior year began, I came back to college re-energized. *This* senior year was going to be much different from my *last* senior year four years ago. Because I had a dorm room all to myself, I mustered up the motivation to retackle the social scene and take on fresh relationships, knowing I could keep my social life separate from my private life.

Still distrustful of females, I was sure that I would be safer hanging out with some not-at-all melodramatic sports guys. Guys could be aggressive and upfront and it would be complemented. I saw them debate sports, literally inches away from fist fighting, then d-i-n-g ... some little "time's-up" bell (audible only to males) rang, which signaled laughing, fist-fiving, and tearing open a case of Natty Light. According to Gail Evans, author of *Play Like a Man, Win Like a Woman*, the common perception of this conduct is not that males are being loud-mouthed, tactless, unruly jerks, but that they are driven and passionate.[123] I simply saw their behavior as "guys being guys." They loved sports so much that they would fight to make their views heard. I wanted that for myself and for other females. I wanted girlfriends, who like my guy friends, didn't complicate their relationships by becoming emotionally anchored to them. Sure, the guys cared about each other, but not in a keep-the-peace-or-die, pet-the-hair-rub-the-back-hand-a-tissue kind of way that girls did. Frankly, by now, I was so sick of girls' contradictory behavior that I only wanted to be a part of the guys' predictable way of communicating. It just seemed better, more productive. Guys didn't seem to stay angry for long, and they could say what was on their mind without having a roommate, teammate, or friend run to another friend to gossip. Even if there was a blowup, they simply knocked the crap out of each other, shook hands, and went on their way. No whispers. No dirty looks. No long, drawn out drama (or so it all seemed at that time).

However, the more time I spent with my male friends, the more I began to notice males participating in relational aggression just as females did. This seemed to happen especially if a guy's "woman" or crush was involved, because the I-think-she's-a-whore/bitch/lesbian-too line and the pretend-like-the-other-girl-is-invisible act could get him laid. There was no where, with no one, that I was safe from relational aggression.

My confidence-sucking, relationship-stealing demon had returned to make sure the fears I had had before entering college were lived out once and for all. Soon enough, I was eating meals and studying by myself. I even dropped out of FCA and The Rock, because I had convinced myself that life in general would be better if I lived it alone. Because the less I was involved, the less relational aggression would stress me out, and the more control I had over it, or so I thought.[124]

Release to Revive

During my senior year of college, I often drove home for the weekend only to enter the perimeters of my native county to become irate. I would try to blow by every mailbox and cow field fast enough not to see anything associated with my past. Yet, even after I had settled in to the peacefulness of my family's hill-hugged acreage, I remained perturbed by my surroundings.

Home was my one safe place. Only it wasn't. Home had not been home for a while. It was supposed to be where I could overindulge on home cooking, where I could trade-in my desk chair and books for the couch and television, where I could sleep through the night sprawled out in my big, soft bed without door-pounding partygoers awakening me. Except, since high school, home had not been a place of total rest and recuperation.

While I did gorge on Mom's specialties, and I did nestle up in front of prime-time dramas, it was not often that I slept soundly. Even as I lay in bed with a pillow wrapped around my head, my walls could not keep out the whooshes of traffic from the nearby highway. It was an annoying reminder that in another day or so I would have to return to college where I would worry about running into Liz, Katie, Bri, Tiffany, Julie, and all of their dirty-look-giving, whispering friends. Yet, the traffic brought an even more disturbing reminder, a reminder that the people of my past would always be close by.

For a while, I had figured that if I could not rid myself of the Honeybees and their followers, I might as well investigate their lives and search for their downfalls. Through Bailey, I stayed updated on who had dropped out of or failed in college, who had dead-end jobs, who had accumulated debt, who had had unplanned pregnancies, and who had developed a less than flattering "beer body." I even skimmed through weeks of local newspapers and court records to find pleasure in my bullies' traffic violations and misdemeanors.

I grew empowered with the revelation of each tidbit of fact or fiction. Convinced that I was putting my journalistic knack to good use, I dreamed of uncovering "big news" that would allow me to turn the tables and obliterate my bullies' reputations.

I was absorbed in finding their screw-ups, but screw-ups were not always what I found. Some of them went on to earn accredited educations, financially rewarding careers, and new cars and homes. And every time I came across one of their commendable achievements, I cursed them, sour that they had received blessings that I felt they did not deserve.

I hardly ever came across the type of information I set out to find. After endless hours spent searching for details that provided nothing more than meager, fruitless seconds of self-satisfaction, I realized I had become the bully my bullies had been to me.

Trip home after trip home, anger saturated and disintegrated my spirit, leaving me exhausted and lonesome. I hated that I hated. I was desperate to extract my secret, deep-rooted emotions, to be rid of competition, envy, and aggression, to return to a state of contentment. Although I had stopped going to my Christian clubs, I had not turned away from God. After feeling the grasp of the Holy Spirit's hands in my dorm room during my sophomore year, I could *never* turn away from God. I was sure He was the only One who would release me from hate's grip. However, the difficulty in allowing God to do this was that I had to fess up to hate's hold on me, and this was not something I readily accepted.

Acts 3:19 told me, "repent, then, and turn to God, so that your sins may be wiped out, that times of refreshing may come from the Lord." Yet, having to acknowledge my behavior to God made my jaw tighten. I had definitely made some decisions that had contradicted my faith. I had mouthed-off, called names, and given stare-downs. I had flipped "the bird." I had thrown punches. I had even considered murder. I could not admit my badness to God! I was scared and embarrassed. Therefore, I kept my mouth shut, and simply allowed the Holy Spirit to intercede in my thinking and prayers.[125]

Slowly, over the next couple of months, I began to see the fallacy of my self-perception, and I realized that I was not a horrible, unhealthy, and immoral person. Since my senior year of high school, I had questioned my integrity because of the false image that the Honeybees had created for me. As a result of my buying into and participating in that image, I also questioned my value. However, it was during my senior year of college, when I read the promises of the New Testament, that I finally forgave myself for my mistakes and my lack of self-worth. At last, I found sweetness in my being bullied.

> Blessed is the [woman] who perseveres under trial, because when [she] has stood the test, [she] will receive the crown of life that God has promised to those who love him. (James 1:12)

The glory of all grace who called you to his eternal glory in Christ, after you suffered a little while, will himself restore you and make you strong, firm and steadfast. (1 Peter 5:10)

Through New Testament verses like these, I realized that I was the same good-hearted, full-of-potential-and-blessings-kind-of-girl that I had always been. Only now, my meaning and hope lasted stronger and longer than it had during all of the time I spent on the basketball court, at award ceremonies, and at fraternity parties where I wildly danced to get attention and acceptance. Now, after realizing my significance in Christ, I saw that my meaning upheld for a lifetime plus an eternity. Christ had already guaranteed my worth when he died for me, and I simply had to embrace that fact.

My mission to restore my vibrancy had just begun, though. The process became daunting when in the height of my excitement I was whammed over and over by numerous verses of forgiveness.

If you forgive [people] when they sin against you, your heavenly Father will also forgive you. But if you do not forgive [people] their sins, your Father will not forgive your sins. (Matthew 6:14–15)

… forgive your brother [and sister] from your heart. (Matthew 18:35)

And when you stand praying, if you hold anything against anyone, forgive him [or her], so that your Father in heaven may forgive you your sins. (Mark 11:24–25)

Forgive, and you will be forgiven. (Luke 6:37)

… forgive and comfort … (2 Corinthians 2:7)

Be kind and compassionate to one another, forgiving each other, just as in Christ God forgave you. (Ephesians 4:32)

… forgive whatever grievances you may have against one another. Forgive as the Lord forgave you. (Colossians 3:13)

Forgive, forgive, forgive. Gag me. "Forgive" began to be all I saw every time I opened my Bible. "Why should I do this?" I asked all the time. *I mean, come on God! I'm no Jesus. I'm not actually capable of this!* I thought. *Did you forget how the Honeybees had hated me, how they had been cruel to me, how they had put me through Hell?!* "Why should *they* be so honored and privileged to receive *my* forgiveness!?"

As far as I was concerned, the only thing that the Honeybees should have received from anyone was the same bullying that I had received from them, the same kind of treatment that would make them know what it felt like to want to kill themselves. I felt that I deserved to see and hear reparation ever before the Honeybees were rewarded! God owed it to me to teach them lessons. Yet, every time I pleaded for Him to take action against them, He said, "No," while I stubbornly waited in false hope and exasperation. I was fuming, and I *always* let God hear about it when I was angry with Him. Over and over, I recited the same, ineffective payback prayers before I finally accepted that I *must* forgive.

Forgiveness seemed to be the only option that would rid me of my burdens. Tired of being anchored to my past and deprived of optimum happiness, I could not deal with hating any longer. If I were to ever accept my situation and benefit from it, I had to quit expecting God to grant me what was not reasonable to be granted. There was no other choice but to give-in to God's way. Only He could deal with my unforgiving attitude, only He could assist and revive me, and I saw this through His Word, which said:

> I will restore you to health and heal your wounds. (Jeremiah 30:17)

> Come to me, all you who are weary and burdened, and I will give you rest. Take my yoke upon you and learn from me, for I am gentle and humble in heart, and you will find rest for your souls. (Matthew 12:20)

Over the course of my senior year, I grew my trust in these promises and again released my prideful, self-dependence and took hold of God-dependent power, but I never felt any abracadabra-smoke-poof-boom transformation. Instead, I was left with inconsistency. Sometimes, I lived to spread love. Other times, I wanted to verbally and physically fight, and if I did not pray to release my aggression, it always stayed. I was flying grounded. In Jesus, I saw an incredible opportunity to ascend above a past that had locked me into my lowest low, but with so much unpredictable emotional weather, I was stuck on standby. I felt like the apostle Paul in Romans 7:15–25:

> I do not understand what I do. For what I want to do I do not do, but what I hate I do. And if I do what I do not want to do, I agree that the law is good. As it is, it is no longer I myself who do it, but it is sin living in me. I know that nothing good lives in me, that is, in my sinful nature. For I have the desire to do what is good, but I cannot carry it out. For what I do is not the good I want to do; no, the evil I do not want to do—this I keep on doing.

Now if I do what I do not want to do, it is no longer I who do it, but it is sin living in me that does it.

So I find this law at work: When I want to do good, evil is right there with me. For in my inner being I delight in God's law, but I see another law at work in the members of my body, waging war against the law of my mind and making me a prisoner of the law of sin at work within my members. What a wretched man I am! Who will rescue me from this body of death? Thanks be to God—through Jesus Christ our Lord!

So then, I myself in my mind am a slave to God's law, but in the sinful nature a slave to the law of sin.

Like Paul, I was a slave to my sinful nature. I tried my darnedest to take off and escape my hatred, but every time I started barreling down the runway, one of my why-did-I-do-that moments shut me down.

After months of swaying back and forth, being delayed by spells of resentment, I was determined never again to disintegrate as I had during and after my previous run-ins with relational aggression. As I incessantly asked the Lord to rescue me from my past, He fueled me and launched me into a sequence of rewards more fulfilling and more enduring than any revenge I could ever carry out or revel in.

It was after a brain-frying afternoon of Economics class that I returned to my computer only to have my mind boggled by an e-mail containing one of those apologies I had thirsted for. It was from Kylee, my former basketball teammate who, in our last game, had stood out on the court and yelled that she could not wait until I left the team because she could not stand me. Kylee said she was sorry for how she had treated me and that she felt as if God wanted her to confess her mistake and ask me for forgiveness. While I was grateful for Kylee's humbleness and compassion and intrigued that faith had connected us, receiving her apology was not as enjoyable as I had hoped. It reminded me of a few times in which I had accidentally taken a drink from a glass of water that I thought was Sprite. My tongue expected fizzy refreshment, but tastelessness caught me off guard. I was always disappointed when that happened. Likewise, my reaction to the apology was not what I thought it would be, and in receiving one "sorry," I lost the need to hear any more. The desperate, needy feeling simply left me.

My fingertips rested on my keyboard, paused by motivating sadness. Here was Kylee telling *me*, "Sorry," when I had made mistakes no better than hers, no better than any of my bullies. All of the sudden, *I* did not deserve forgiveness. I was so flawed and undeserving, a natural mistake making machine, capable of so much hate that, at one point, I even hated the very person that died for me. Yet, Jeremiah 31:34, "For I will forgive [your] wickedness and will remember [your] sins no more," assured me that, despite my feelings of unworthiness, I had still received God's forgiveness.[126] And it was not just words on paper that gave me this assurance. It was a sensation in the depth of my core, a feeling that came whenever I prayed for my anger and guilt to be lifted, a feeling that made the muscles in my chest, shoulders, and arms peacefully weaken, and a feeling that only happened when I asked God for forgiveness.

Grateful for God's limitless mercy more than ever, I confessed out-loud to the Lord that I had been wrong to authorize Satan to suck-away my esteem, thrive on my dejection, and trap me in a vicious current of abhorrence. For too long I had been overcome by evil. It was time that I defeated evil with good, and so, I first forgave myself then typed on and forgave Kylee.[127] However, not long after I accepted Kylee's apology, I underwent another nosedive.

Immediately following my college graduation, I moved back home until I could find a job. After about a month, I started to become comfortable with being seen in town again. I went to the gym, restaurants, the library; I even stepped back into the mall a few times. This was during the same time that I had actually started to tolerate hearing myself say, "I forgive them." Then suddenly, I was whammed again.

I thought I would need resuscitated as, one night when I was praying for the Honeybees, the words, "I know I've gotta love 'em," awkwardly rolled out of my mouth. For some time, Bible verses that encouraged me to love my enemies had hounded me, and I always passed them off as nonsense.

Love your neighbor [even if they're a bully] as yourself. (Leviticus 19:18)

Love your enemies and pray for those who persecute you, that you may be sons [and daughters] of your Father in heaven. (Matthew 5:44–45)

Love your enemies, do good to those who hate you, bless those who curse you, pray for those who mistreat you ... and lend to them without expecting to get anything back. (Luke 6:27–35)

Love one another.... You must love one another. (John 13:34)

This is my command: Love each other. (John 15:17)

Be devoted to one another in brotherly [and sisterly] love. (Romans 12:10)

Let no debt remain outstanding, except the continuing debt to love one another. (Romans 13:8)

Serve one another in love. (Galatians 5:13)

… Live a life of love, just as Christ loved us … (Ephesians 5:2)

Above all, love each other deeply, because love covers a multitude of sins. (1 Peter 4:8)

We should love one another. (1 John 3:11)

Gag me again. *God, you canNOT be serious*! I noiselessly screamed. *"I forgive them" … okay … but not "I love them!"* Love meant intimacy. *Don't make me do this*, I pleaded. It was much easier to write-off the Honeybees and to go my own way and forget them.[128] Unfortunately, I could never *really* forget them or what they had done to me and how their treatment had made me feel.

Ironically, in the midst of this inner struggle, several encounters with Chelsea, my former Honeybee gymnastics teammate, refreshed my painful past. I had always been worried about running into the Honeybees. I prayed that if it ever happened God would help me maintain calmness, and I saw and felt Him grant me my request during my unexpected meetings with Chelsea.

Chelsea was the only Honeybee I had seen since I graduated from high school. Since I had returned home from college, I had seen her about five times in the matter of two or three weeks, everywhere from local pizza shops to restaurants and at grocery stores. We always saw each other from a distance, but it still appeared that a civil conversation could not occur, as Chelsea was visibly over-taken by adrenaline, destructive emotion, and sin, just as I had been many times before. Surprisingly, I was not tempted to respond to her (not to say that her dirty looks and unkindly statements did not hurt or bother me). I did not even feel angry with Chelsea. I simply walked away every time, seeing myself in her and wanting better for both of us. After every encounter, Jesus' words, "Father, forgive them, for they do not know what they are doing," briefed my mind, pro-ducing a compassionate sadness.[129] It had to be the same kind of sadness that God had had for me when I had been insubordinate—the same kind of sadness that He still had for me as I resisted loving Chelsea, Sara, Bri, and all of the other people from my past.

A critical component of my faith was missing. This significant character glitch had me disrespecting God's Word and living in darkness, blind to my faith's potential.[130] However, this time, my flaw did not slow my pace. Once again, I centered my emotions with God and trusting in His directions, I powered through the headwinds and jetted onward.

Although I had not seen any of the other Honeybees since high school, I anticipated a Chelsea-like reaction from them too. Being friends or even at-a-distance associates with any of them seemed impossible. How was I supposed to love people who made themselves so hard to love? If only they would chip-in and chill-out long enough to hear me out, they might re-evaluate their views of me, and they might be able to accept my forgiveness of them and also forgive me for the hatred I held toward them. That would make healing a lot easier! Sadly, they did not have to involve themselves in any way, and I could not force them to either. So, if they did not want to partake in love, how could I still obey God's instructions? Was it even possible to love them if they never loved me in return? Why not? God had loved me even though, in my past, I had angrily, ignorantly, and repeatedly lashed out at Him.

While God did not show me face-to-face, in-the-flesh love, He graciously extended it to me in many other beautiful ways. Without His stillness, I would not have seen the disruption within me. Without His patience, I would not have been able to work through my disturbance. Without His forgiveness, I would not have been able to forgive myself, then others, and, without His love, I would not have healed as much as I had at this point.

As precious creations of God and as my sisters and brothers in Christ, my bullies deserved as much stillness, patience, mercy, and compassion as I could possibly share.

Although, upon choosing to love the Honeybees and their followers, I did not feel like mowing them over with hugs and kisses, I sincerely wanted to not only think and talk better about them, but to do better for them. Like the affection God displayed toward me, my love for them did not necessarily require my physical presence, but through devoted prayer, without them knowing, I could support them in their struggles and embrace their blessings.

And so, just like I had in my Lazyboy during my sophomore year of college, I stretched out my arms to Jesus, so He could extract my every last bit of anger and bitterness, so I could give my bullies and myself the best love I could offer. Throughout the entire summer, the more I stretched, the more I released, and the more I revived until my lack of like was replaced with loads of love.

Closing

Forgiving and loving our aggressors can be challenging, especially for females, because we tend to completely write-off our dysfunctional and failed relationships. We all view, experience, and implement forgiveness and love differently. For some of us, releasing debts or asking for mercy comes easily. It might only take a few weeks or a couple months to do so. For others, it might take a number of years, if not a lifetime. Some of us feel that re-engaging in and "doing business" with past relationships would be harmful to our healing and wellbeing. Some of us have no choice but to re-enter broken relationships, relationships in which relational aggression will likely resurface. Some of us feel the need to express forgiveness to the person or people that have caused us pain, and some of us clear our consciences by seeking forgiveness from those we have hurt. Yet, what is similar for all of us is that in order to forgive, ask for forgiveness, and move forward in respectable compassion, we must bring our hurts to the surface and deal with them, as difficult and uncomfortable as that may be.[131]

For me, forgiveness was not an easy, instant task; sometimes it was downright grueling and painful. My forgiveness was not a cover-up or an act of "womanly duty" in order to get along with everyone or to act as if I was everyone's friend (that, I have learned, is an impossible undertaking). Rather it was a heartfelt, truly desired, incremental and devoted process that took place over a nearly five-year span. In fact, it continues to take place as I dig up buried issues, face still-tender issues, and meet even new issues. Although sometimes it has been tempting to track-down Sara and the Honeybees, convey my forgiveness to them, and express my need to be forgiven, I have avoided doing so. Instead, I have learned that my most productive option is to declare my forgiveness to God on a daily basis. In doing so, I am able to reduce my pride, evaluate my insecurities and roles, manage my emotions and my perceptions of past and current relationships, and, most importantly, practice giving the same abundant forgiveness to the Honeybees that God has given me. Because despite whom my bullies have been or who they are, or what they have done to me or other people, they, like me, should be entitled to make mistakes without receiving a social trashing. We all deserve to be forgiven, we deserve the freedom to live without the pain of our pasts and without fear of social contamination and failure, and we deserve to forgive ourselves for any role we have played in relational aggression.

I am grateful that God has granted me boundless mercy, because in dealing with female bullying, I have certainly made more than enough public and private mistakes. There were times when I failed to find a healthy, necessary balance between silence and eruption. There were times when I should have tossed aside popularity and sought justice. Times when I was overtaken by timidity and afraid of confrontation. Times when I came on so strong that I missed the opportunity to have an effective impact. Throughout my healing, there were times when I remained sexist against other females and unrealistic in my expectations of them (and of people in general). There were times when I myself resorted to relational aggression. There were times when I chose isolation because it seemed safer than group participation. There were times when I physically and emotionally hit the ground and stayed there for a while. To present day, there are still times when I am frustrated and impatient by my limitations and other females' limitations. However, perhaps what has been most difficult of all, are the times when I am required to participate in relationships that I would much rather dismiss, relationships in which I fear being targeted and retaliating against the people who target me.

Relationships can hurt, especially when we encounter toxic rivalry and indirect aggression within them. Relationships are what connect and strengthen us, yet separate and weaken us.[132] Relationships open us up to vulnerability and attack. Through them, we are offended and damaged, but we are also able to practice realness by sifting through our irritations, anger, envies, and rivalries of each other so that we can discuss them with each other and learn how to cope with aggression effectively. Being able to forgive another girl or woman after we have been bullied is not usually a comfortable thing to do, but if we do not forgive, we have no future for our relationships.[133] Rebuilding respect and consistently putting ourselves back out there, socially and intimately, can be a challenging task, but it is the chance we must take, if not just for ourselves, then for other girls and women. Because it is in relationships that our touchdowns turn into liftoffs, that our hurt transforms into growth, and that our failures become successes.

Ladies, let us not kid ourselves. As females, we own a kind of social power, and we must hold ourselves and each other accountable when we abuse it. We must resist judging, stereotyping, gossiping, harshly criticizing, insulting, name-calling, and building alliances against each other, and we must locate our sources of anger, examine our motives, confront our pressures and limitations, and arrive at workable compromises.

I am not proposing that we extinguish our competitive spirits; that would be detrimental to our future. However, I am recommending that we set realistic standards in our rivalries and transform our meaning of aggression and competition. As I have found, we are not free of conflict, and we have to understand that competition often contains conflict. If conflict is articulated productively and directly, it and all of its accompanying emotions, is healthy. Nor are we morally above anger, envy, and opposition. We merely own all of these emotions on different individual levels, and we should not feel guilty or awkward to possess these natural feelings. Expressing these emotions does not mean we are insensitive, cold, impersonal, ungrateful, unfeminine, or irreligious. Rather, it signals a meaningful sense of involvement and identification, and it indicates the magnitude and strength of our ambitions and desires.[134] However, if we do not channel our aggressive and competitive emotions into proper outlets, and instead we hold them in to fester or leave them to brew within our social networks, then relational aggression will continue to manifest.

We must realize that female competitors do not have to be enemies, and female competition does not have to be taboo.[135] There are a lot of girls and women who like competing. I am one of them, but I do not enjoy competition at the expense of another female's confidence and reputation. I know that it hurts when other girls and women target me in this way, and because of this, I wish for no girl or woman to be crushed because she pursued and attained her dreams and desires.

We must also realize that we do not always have to get along or create the illusion that we get along. Some of us just plain do not like each other, some of us never will, and some of us will always be competitors against one another, but this does not mean that we cannot respect each other and communally work to alter our circumstances. We must support each other's determination and the different paces at which we achieve individual successes, because when one of us moves forward, we pave new pathways for all of us. We have to understand that it is not bad to openly express our wants and go after our aspirations. For so long, we have held the belief that ambition is negative, because society has always told us it is unladylike. It is our common belief that, as a gender, we must either stay in the same place together or move forward together, never as separate individuals, because this means we are abandoning, betraying, and placing ourselves above our own kind. We need to dispel this perception, and this can be done by applying positive connotations of competitiveness and directness to women just as they are applied to men. Once we achieve this, we can honestly and realistically convey what we want out of our relationships, and we can deal with our rivalries and communicate in an easier and more normal, productive way.[136]

If we cannot challenge or confront each other or live-out our own separate identities, how will we grow stronger personally and universally? Healthy competition and honest, direct communication is needed if we are to produce and attain new and higher spiritual, psychological, social, economic, political, academic, and athletic levels, but if we resort to relational bullying in order to get the things we want, we will only ground and limit ourselves and other females.[137]

Therefore, we must gear our aggression and competition around improving our own personal performances, and we must use our frustrations as motivation to lift-up other females. We can do this by emotionally and physically experiencing the unique blessings God has given us and by recognizing and embracing the blessings He gives to others. If we do not find an encouraging resource to humble our minds and fill us with what we lack, we will suffer a lifetime of reservation and insecurity. We will be constrained by an inexhaustible cycle of competition in which Satan uses us to attack one another doggedly. It is he who wants our envy to turn into hate. He wants us to stay angry, to retaliate, to mistrust, to mistreat, to write each other off, to drown in never-ending self-doubt and depression, and to roll right into the hanger and put our lives in park, because it is when we participate in female bullying and dwell on its viciousness that we pay a costly price. We stop seeing hope in our relationships, and we are drawn away from the hope that Christ gives us.

Despite our differences or desire for sameness, we are all God's daughters. We do not have to one-up or undercut each other or even-out with each other in order to win His attention and love. He does not prefer one of us to the other. He does not favor blondes to brunettes, D-cups to A-cups, size two to size twenty-two, BMWs to Buicks, or 15,000 square foot houses to 1,500 square foot houses. We place enormous moral and material significance upon winning these game pieces and withholding them from other girls and women, but the ownership of these objects matter nothing to God. He does not require us to tear other females apart with gossip, dirty looks, silent treatments, and other indirect actions in order to gain His admiration. He does not even expect us to get along all the time, but He does require us to respect and forgive each other, and in that sense, "respect" and "forgive" define loving one another. Loving other females in this way, however, requires a great deal of self-love, which can be truly and lastingly found in Jesus Christ and, in turn, carried into our acquaintanceships.

Once we find our beauty, compassion, strength, and purpose, untouched by the world's rigid standards, we will not have to resort to punishing and shaming each other because we are afraid that another girl or woman's success will cause us less acceptance or make us look less feminine.[138] It is in Jesus that we can focus on holding power *with* each other rather than holding power *over* each other. It is in Him that one's building respect for other females becomes a foreseeable, workable option. It is in Him that we are given a positive, supportive, and encouraging belief system to connect our experiences and worth. It is in Him that we are linked to something larger and more precious than the issues that occur in our lives and in our communities. And it is in Him, no matter whom we are or how we stack up against other females, that we triumph.[139]

Let us not be too frightened to further this conversation. There is nothing wrong with direct confrontation and personal communication. If we do not talk, we simply will not be heard, and we will not facilitate change. However, our efforts should not be satisfied in talking and telling alone. Now, we must analyze our roles, prepare, and implement methods that allow us to deal with this cultural dilemma. In doing so, we will better anticipate our problems, and we will respond differently to conflict so we do not cause each other emotional detriment, discourage each other from succeeding, or deny each other from receiving help.[140]

Calling out covert aggression might require us to unearth painful memories, stand up to our own Queen Bees and their cliques, or step down from our own abusive positions. It could very well mean that we will have to disengage from unhealthy friendships, leave job positions, or be outcast by family and friends. Standing against indirect aggression can be quite scary. It requires guts. Yet, if we keep failing to act, we will continue to set ourselves up for relational failure and teach our sisters, our daughters, and ourselves to value relational bullying.

I have been blessed to hear apologies from people who I thought I would never hear say "sorry"—including Honeybee Chelsea, whom to I returned my own "sorry." I have encountered former schoolmates that I thought I would never be able to bear seeing again—including Honeybees Sara, Amber, Melissa, and Kara. And I have ventured to places I thought I would never be able to return—including the grounds of my high school. However, even as I overcome obstructions, I continue to struggle with personal limitations.

Presently, in my social, professional, and spiritual life, there are times that I am tempted to keep quiet about relational aggression, times that I pretend that I do not care and that I am not affected by the actions I witness and the words I hear. It is the easiest way to avoid being personally attacked and becoming discouraged, but it is also the easiest way to solve nothing.

Because I am frequently harassed and bothered by female bullying, I still sometimes encounter moments in which my emotions take a dive. However, I no longer allow myself to hit pavement and come to a halt, because the Lord Almighty, who cannot be mocked, pilots my life.[141] With Him, I cannot be alienated, intimidated, or ruined by female bullying. With Him, I accelerate and ascend. With Him, I am fueled and flying.

Once we seriously consider female bullying a problem, we will be able to educate ourselves about the reasons for its occurrence, evaluate our own roles, and understand others' roles. Then, we will not have to be tortured by relational aggression or see it as a result of our personal failures or our gender's failures. With assurance and security in God, we do not need relational aggression to further our individual or group purpose. Let us find self-confidence, self-love, security, and courage through Jesus Christ so that when a fellow female achieves great things we embrace her instead of crash her momentum. Let us not barrel down the runway, toward our capabilities, only to be stopped by relational aggression and grounded from achieving greatness. Let us be empowered by the ability to assert ourselves over female bullying, form healthy disagreements, and either improve our relationships or extract ourselves from their abusiveness. Only then, will we conceptualize the true strength of the female identity. Only then will we leave the ground and fly.

Source Notes

1. Bly, Laura. "The real *Laguna Beach* disdains its MTV image." *USA Today* 3 Mar. 2006: 1A.

2. Fillion, Kate. *Lip Service: The Truth About Women's Darker Side in Love, Sex, and Friendship*. New York: Harper Collins, 1996, p.39.

3. Crick, Nicki R. and Jennifer K. Grotpeter. "Relational Aggression, Gender, and Social-Psychological Adjustment." *Child Development* 66 (1995): 710–722; Crick, Nicki R. and Nicole Werner. "Relational Aggression and Social-Psychological Adjustment in a College Sample." *Journal of Abnormal Psychology* 108 (1999): 615–619; http://www.opheliaproject.org/main/relational_aggression.htm. The Ophelia Project. Erie, PA.

4. Coyne, Sarah, John Archer, and Mike Eslea. "Cruel intentions on television and in real life: Can viewing indirect aggression increase viewers' subsequent indirect aggression?" *Journal of Experimental Child Psychology* 88 (2004): 250; www.relationalaggression.net.

5. Angier, Natalie. "Spiking the punch: In defense of female aggression." *Woman: An Intimate Geography*. Boston: Houghton and Mifflin, 1999.

6. Crick, Nicki R. and Jennifer K. Grotpeter. "Relational Aggression, Overt Aggression, and Friendship." *Child Development* 67 (1996): 2328–2338; Mounts, Nina S. "What About Girls? Are They Really Not Aggressive?" *The Ohio State University Human Development and Family Life Bulletin: A Review of Research and Practice* 3 (1997).

7. Bjorkqvist, Kaj, Kristi M.J. Lagerspetz, and Ari Kaukiainen. "Do Girls Manipulate and Boys Fight? Developmental Trends in Regard to Direct and Indirect Aggression." *Aggressive Behavior* 18 (1992): 117–127.

8. Crick, Nicki R. and Jennifer K. Grotpeter. "Relational Aggression, Gender, and Social-Psychological Adjustment." *Child Development* 66 (1995): 710–722; Bjorkvist, Kai, Karin Osterman, and Kirsti Langerspetz. "Sex Differ-

ences in Covert Aggression Among Adults." *Aggressive Behavior* 20 (1994): 27–33; Crick, Nicki R. and Nicole Werner. "Relational Aggression and Social-Psychological Adjustment in a College Sample." *Journal of Abnormal Psychology* 108 (1999): 615–619; Dellasega, Cheryl and Charisse Nixon. *Girl Wars: 12 Strategies That Will End Female Bullying*. New York: Simon and Schuster, 2003, p.2; Linder, Jennifer, Nicki Crick, and Andrew Collins. "Relational Aggression and Victimization in Young Adults' Romantic Relationships." *Social Development* 11 (2002): 69–86.

9.   Simmons, Rachel. *Odd Girl Out: The Hidden Culture of Aggression in Girls*. New York: Harcourt, 2002, p.16.

10. U.S. Department of Labor, Bureau of Labor Statistics. "(Unadj) Civilian Labor Force—Women (1971 to Present). Series ID: LNU01000002, 2005. From 1971 to 2004, the number of women in the workforce doubled; U.S. Department of Labor, Bureau of Labor Statistics. "Employment Status of the Civilian Population 16 Years and Over by Sex 1971 to Date." 2002. From 1971 to 1991, the number of women in the workforce climbed from 32 million to 57 million. Plus more women were pursuing full-time careers like law, engineering, and medicine, which were usually reserved for men; The Woman's Sports Foundation. "Women's Sports Foundation 2002 Annual Report." 2002. In 1972, the year Title IX passed, seven percent of high school and 15 percent of college athletes were women, and by the year 2002, that number had rose to 41 percent high school and 42 percent college female athletes.

11. Fillion, Kate. *Lip Service: The Truth About Women's Darker Side in Love, Sex, and Friendship*. New York: Harper Collins, 1996, p.50.

12. Gilligan, Carol. *In a Different Voice*. Cambridge: Harvard University Press, 1982, p.8.

13. Barash, Susan Shapiro. *Tripping the Prom Queen: The Truth About Women and Rivalry*. New York: St. Martin's Press, 2006; Campbell, Anne. *Men, Women, and Aggression: From Rage in Marriage to Violence in the Streets—How Gender Affects the Way We Act*. New York: Basic Books, 1993; Eichenbaum, Luise, and Susie Orbach. *Between Women: Love, Envy, and Competition in Women's Friendships*. New York: Viking, 1998, p.89; Fillion,

Kate. *Lip Service: The Truth About Women's Darker Side in Love, Sex, and Friendship*. New York: Harper Collins, 1996, p.24, 30–31, 35.

14. Mooney, Nan. *I Can't Believe She Did That! Why Women Betray Other Women at Work*. New York: St. Martin's Press, 2005, p.51.

15. Dellasega, Cheryl. *Mean Girls Grown Up: Adult Women Who are Still Queen Bees, Middle Bees, and Afraid-to-Bees*. Hoboken: Wiley, 2005.

16. Barash, Susan Shapiro. *Tripping the Prom Queen: The Truth About Women and Rivalry*. New York: St. Martin's Press, 2006, p.15; Osterman, Karin. "Cross-cultural evidence of female indirect aggression." *Aggressive Behavior* 24 (1998) p.1–8; Simmons, Rachel. *Odd Girl Out: The Hidden Culture of Aggression in Girls*. New York: Harcourt, 2002, p.16–18, 124–127.

17. Dellasega, Cheryl and Charisse Nixon. *Girls Wars: 12 Strategies That Will End Female Bullying*. New York: Simon and Schuster, 2003, p.3; Simmons, Rachel. *Odd Girl Out: The Hidden Culture of Aggression in Girls*. New York: Harcourt, 2002, p.16–17, 37, 250; Wiseman, Rosalind. *Queen Bees and Wannabees: Helping Your Daughter Survive Cliques, Gossip, Boyfriends, and Other Realities of Adolescence*. Three Rivers Press: New York, 2002, p.23–24; Chesler, Phyllis. *Woman's Inhumanity to Woman*. New York: Thunder's Mouth Press, 2000.

18. Campbell, Anne. *Men, Women, and Aggression: From Rage in Marriage to Violence in the Streets—How Gender Affects the Way We Act*. New York: Basic Books, 1993, p.38.

19. Evans, Gail. *Play Like a Man, Win Like a Woman: What Men Know About Success That Women Need to Learn*. Broadway Books, New York: 2000, p.67.

20. Wiseman, Rosalind. *Queen Bees and Wannabes: Helping Your Daughter Survive Cliques, Gossip, Boyfriends and Other Realities of Adolescence*. Three Rivers Press: New York, 2002, p.20, 24.

21. Adler, Patricia and Peter Adler. "Dynamics of Inclusion and Exclusion in Preadolescent Cliques," *Social Psychology Quarterly* 58 (1995): 145–161.

22. Campbell, Anne. *Men, Women, and Aggression: From Rage in Marriage to Violence in the Streets—How Gender Affects the Way We Act.* New York: Basic Books, 1993, p.76; Rosalind Wiseman *Queen Bees and Wannabes: Helping Your Daughter Survive Cliques, Gossip, Boyfriends and Other Realities of Adolescence.* Three Rivers Press: New York, 2002, p.19.

23. Campbell, Anne. *Women, and Aggression: From Rage in Marriage to Violence in the Streets—How Gender Affects the Way We Act.* New York: Basic Books, 1993, p.34; Bjorkqvist, Kaj, Kristi M.J. Lagerspetz, and Ari Kaukiainen, "Do Girls Manipulate and Boys Fight? Developmental Trends in Regard to Direct and Indirect Aggression," *Aggressive Behavior* 18 (1992): 117–127.

24. Goodman, Ellen and Patricia O'Brien. *I Know Just What You Mean: The Power of Friendship in Women's Lives.* New York: Simon and Schuster, 2000.

25. Campbell, Anne. *Men, Women, and Aggression: From Rage in Marriage to Violence in the Streets—How Gender Affects the Way We Act.* New York: Basic Books, 1993, p.33, 34; Ely, Robin. "The Effects of Organizational Demographics and Social Identity on Relationships among Professional Women." *Administrative Science Quarterly* 39 (1994); Wiseman, Rosalind. *Queen Bees and Wannabes: Helping Your Daughter Survive Cliques, Gossip, Boyfriends and Other Realities of Adolescence.* Three Rivers Press: New York, 2002.

26. Adler, Patricia and Peter Adler. "Dynamics of Inclusion and Exclusion in Preadolescent Cliques," *Social Psychology Quarterly* 58 (1995): 151, 158.

27. Ibid p.152; Dellasega, Cheryl and Charisse Nixon. *Girls Wars: 12 Strategies That Will End Female Bullying.* New York: Simon and Schuster, 2003, p.8.

28. Dittmann, Melissa. "Anger across the gender division: Researchers strive to understand how men and women experience and express anger." *American Psychological Association* 34 (2003): 52.

29. Adler, Patricia and Peter Adler. "Dynamics of Inclusion and Exclusion in Preadolescent Cliques," *Social Psychology Quarterly* 58 (1995): 152–156.

30. Descriptions of adult alliances slightly differ from adolescent cliques. To better understand grown-up cliques and the roles both women and men play in them, refer to Rosalind Wiseman's *Queen Bee Moms and Kingpin Dads:*

Dealing with the Parents, Teachers, Coaches, and Counselors who can make—or Break—Your Child's Future. New York: Crown, 2006.

31. Merten, Don E. "The Meaning of Meanness: Popularity, Competition, and Conflict Among Junior High School Girls." *Sociology of Education* 70 (1997): 180.

32. Russell, Alan and Laurence Owens. "Peer estimates of school-aged boys' and girls' aggression to same—and cross-sex targets." *Social Development* 8 (1999): 365–79.

33. Dittmann, Melissa. "Anger across the gender division: Researchers strive to understand how men and women experience and express anger." *American Psychological Association* 34 (2003): 52.

34. Wiseman, Rosalind. *Queen Bees and Wannabes: Helping Your Daughter Survive Cliques, Gossip, Boyfriends and Other Realities of Adolescence.* Three Rivers Press: New York, 2002, p.25–36.

35. Caroline Arnold. *Birds: Nature's Magnificent Flying Machines.* Watertown: Charlesbridge Publishing, 2003.

36. Wiseman, Rosalind. *Queen Bee Moms and Kingpin Dads: Dealing with the Parents, Teachers, Coaches, and Counselors who can make—or Break—Your Child's Future.* New York: Crown, 2006, p.6–7, 28, 96, 223. There is a competition in "Perfect Parent World" too, where many adults "measure themselves against an impossible standard and imagine that the moms and dads with the most power and highest social status" are the families with the right house, the right careers, the right clothes, the priciest cars, and the most well behaved children. This is the type of competition that "lays the foundation for adults mistreating one another—and our children—and prevents parents from having good relationships with one another."

37. Curtis Theron Williams. *The Ten Commandments.* Curtis Theron Williams Publisher. 1969. This scene depicts Exodus 1, which refers to Pharaoh's effort to kill newborn Hebrew boys. Because the Hebrew midwives feared God, they lied to Pharaoh in order to save babies. However, their lie was righteous rather than vicious. Therefore, the relation of William's illustration in regard to the commandment is open to interpretation.

38. Wiseman, Rosalind. *Queen Bee Moms and Kingpin Dads: Dealing with the Parents, Teachers, Coaches, and Counselors who can make—or Break—Your Child's Future*. New York: Crown, 2006, p.93. In religious communities, people often think that they share the same morals with everyone in their congregation. When this doesn't turn out to be the case, it can feel like a harsh betrayal.

39. Merten, Don E. "The Meaning of Meanness: Popularity, Competition, and Conflict Among Junior High School Girls." *Sociology of Education* 70 (1997): 181. "During sixth grade attractiveness to boys became increasingly important."

40. Johnston, Marc A. and Charles B. Crawford. "Stigmatizing women's aggressive behavior: Who does it benefit and why?" *Behavioral and Brain Sciences* 22 (1999): 226 227. "Aggressive women or women in positions of authority are generally disliked and shunned by other women." Yet, even in this case aggressive girls tend to be popular (Merten 177).

41. Simmons, Rachel. *Odd Girl Out: The Hidden Culture of Aggression in Girls*. New York: Harcourt, 2002, p.118. This rejection results because society thinks that "openly competitive behavior undermines the "good girl" personality," and in this sense, competition among girls is viewed negatively as "a desire to be better than others," to be "all that," and to deny others from attaining what you want for yourself.

42. Pipher, Mary. *Reviving Ophelia: Saving the Selves of Adolescent Girls*. New York: Ballantine, 1994, p.68. "Girls punish other girls for failing to achieve the same impossible goals that they are failing to achieve."

43. Adler, Patricia and Peter Adler. "Dynamics of Inclusion and Exclusion in Preadolescent Cliques," *Social Psychology Quarterly* 58 (1995): 155.

44. Simmons, Rachel. *Odd Girl Out: The Hidden Culture of Aggression in Girls*. New York: Harcourt, 2002, p.43, 44, 79–84.

45. Ibid p.16. "Girls target you where they know you're weakest."

46. Brown, Lyn Mikel. Paper presented at the annual MESCA conference, 8 November, 2001, and for the greater Portland Girls Collaborative, 19

March, 2002. Excerpted from Lyn Mikel Brown's *Girlfighting: Betrayal, Teasing and Rejection Among Girls.*

47. Simmons, Rachel. *Odd Girl Out: The Hidden Culture of Aggression in Girls.* New York: Harcourt, 2002, p.71–75, 79–84.

48. www.apa/org/monitor/oct02/bullying.html "Attackers are rarely impulsive. They planned their actions."

49. Simmons, Rachel. *Odd Girl Out: The Hidden Culture of Aggression in Girls.* New York: Harcourt, 2002, p.82. "Alliance building is a sign of peer affirmation, an unspoken contract that means, for the moment anyway that a girl will not be abandoned. If she can turn everyone against a target, it is impossible for them to turn against her."

50. Benenson, Joyce F., and Deborah Bennaroch. "Gender differences in response to friends' hypothetical greater success." *Journal of Early Adolescence* 18 (1998): 192–208. This study found that girls became upset if one of their friends were in any way superior to them. If the girls felt that a friend was too successful they might abandon the relationship.

51. Adler, Patricia and Peter Adler. "Dynamics of Inclusion and Exclusion in Preadolescent Cliques," *Social Psychology Quarterly* 58 (1995): 151, 153, 154.

52. Wiseman, Rosalind. *Queen Bees and Wannabes: Helping Your Daughter Survive Cliques, Gossip, Boyfriends and Other Realities of Adolescence.* Three Rivers Press: New York, 2002, p.25–36; Simmons, Rachel. *Odd Girl Out: The Hidden Culture of Aggression In Girls.* New York: Harcourt, 2002, p.79–84.

53. Ibid, p.79, 80.

54. Rose, Amanda, Lance P. Swenson, and Erika M. Waller. "Among young teens, aggression equals popularity." *Developmental Psychology* 40 (2004): 378–387.

55. Merten, Don E. "The Meaning of Meanness: Popularity, Competition, and Conflict Among Junior High School Girls." *Sociology of Education* 70 (1997): 184. "As the popularity of one girl increases, the popularity of another decreases."

56. Simmons, Rachel. *Odd Girl Out: The Hidden Culture of Aggression in Girls*. New York: Harcourt, 2002, p.103–120.

57. Astor, Ron Avi, Heather Meyer, and William Behre. "Unowned Places and Times: Maps and Interviews About Violence in High Schools." *American Educational Research Journal* 36 (1999): 3–42. "Violence tends to occur in areas such as hallways, playgrounds, restrooms, and cafeterias during non academic time periods."

58. Crowley Jack, Dana. *Behind the Mask: Destruction and Creativity in Women's Aggression*. Cambridge: Harvard University Press, 1999, p.282. "Certain types of looks—steely eyed hatred, cold, disdain—are ways of delivering aggression indirectly. Eyes can express powerful emotions and intentions, such as a determination to hurt or destroy another. One can always deny the intent or feeling behind a malignant stare, and this makes it a relatively safe means to deliver hostility ... Verbal expressions reveal the persisting belief that the eye carries malevolent power: "if looks could kill, he would be dead." Eyes "burn holes" in others, people "look daggers," glances are sharp, penetrating, keen, deadly. The fear that the eye has the power to injure or to alter reality is captured in "evil eye" superstitions. Women tried as witches were often accused of looking at others in a harmful way. Cross-culturally, people share the idea that the human eye penetrates or pierces, and that it can invade personal space;" Owens, Lawrence, Rosalyn Shute, and Phillip Slee. "'Guess what I just heard!' Indirect aggression among teenage girls in Australia." *Aggressive Behavior* 26 (2000): 67–83. Girls "spread rumors, break confidences, and criticize others' clothing, appearance, or personality." They "say nasty things, barely audible, about a girl who is sitting a few seats ahead." They use "code names in plotting against others," and harass each other by giggling loudly, writing and passing mean notes, being sarcastic, making prank phone calls, staring, and soliciting classmates and adults for support against their target; Brown, Lyn Mikel. Paper presented at the annual MESCA conference, 8 November, 2001, and for the greater Portland Girls Collaborative, 19 March, 2002. Excerpted from Lyn Mikel Brown's *Girlfighting: Betrayal, Teasing and Rejection Among Girls*. "Labeling other girls sluts doesn't necessarily have anything to do with sex or sexual behavior, but is a way for girls to seek revenge or to control another girl who is too different or too popular or threatening in some way ... Girls and women derogate and judge and reject other girls and women for the same reasons they fear being derogated and judged and rejected—for not match-

ing up to the ideals of beauty and behavior or for being brave enough not to care." Townsend, John M. and Timothy Wasserman. "The perception of sexual attractiveness: Sex differences in variability." *Archives of Sexual Behavior* 26 (1997): 243–68. "A common method of making someone appear less attractive is to derogate, slight, and insult them … women criticized other women's physical appearance, and implied either that they were promiscuous or that they were sexual teases." If a woman feels she cannot make herself more attractive, she will compete with another woman by using this technique to make her opponent look less attractive. This also calls into question the target's ability to be sexually monogamous.

59. Barash, Susan Shapiro. *Tripping the Prom Queen: The Truth About Women and Rivalry.* New York: St. Martin's Press, 2006, p.41; Men punish those who are weak while women punish those who are strong; Pipher, Mary. *Reviving Ophelia: Saving the Selves of Adolescent Girls.* New York: Ballantine, 1994, p.68. Girls "punish by picking a certain girl, usually one who is relatively happy, and making her life miserable."

60. Fillion, Kate. *Lip Service: The Truth About Women's Darker Side in Love, Sex, and Friendship.* New York: Harper Collins, 1996, p.52; Wiseman, Rosalind. *Queen Bee Moms and Kingpin Dads: Dealing with the Parents, Teachers, Coaches, and Counselors who can make—or Break—Your Child's Future.* New York: Crown, 2006, p.136. People tend to use phrases like "don't stoop to their level," "kill them with kindness," and "turn the other cheek" as excuses to shy away from confrontation or assert moral superiority over someone.

61. Adler, Patricia and Peter Adler. "Dynamics of Inclusion and Exclusion in Preadolescent Cliques," *Social Psychology Quarterly* 58 (1995): 155, 158. "Many clique members relished the opportunity to go along with such exclusive activities, welcoming the feelings of privilege, power, and inclusion. Other appreciated the absence of ridicule toward themselves." Members "submit to the dominance of clique leaders in order to earn a share of their reflected status and position."

62. Wiseman, Rosalind. *Queen Bees and Wannabes: Helping Your Daughter Survive Cliques, Gossip, Boyfriends and Other Realities of Adolescence.* Three Rivers Press: New York, 2002, p.27–31, 33, 34.

63. Campbell, Anne. *Men, Women, and Aggression: From Rage in Marriage to Violence in the Streets—How Gender Affects the Way We Act.* New York: Basic Books, 1993, p.26, 38.

64. Pipher, Mary. *Reviving Ophelia: Saving the Selves of Adolescent Girls.* Ballantine: New York, 1994.

65. Sands, Sarah. "Do You Dress for Men or Women?" *Harper's Bazaar* Aug. 2004; Barash, Susan Shapiro. *Tripping the Prom Queen: The Truth About Women and Rivalry.* New York: St. Martin's Press, 2006, p.111. When it comes to sex appeal, female rivalry can become more heated than ever.

66. Astor, Ron Avi, Heather Meyer, and William Behre. "Unowned Places and Times: Maps and Interviews About Violence in High Schools." *American Educational Research Journal* 36 (1999): 3–42. "Violence tends to occur in areas such as hallways, playgrounds, restrooms, and cafeterias during non academic time periods."

67. Cowan, Gloria, C. Neighbors, J. DeLaMoreaux, and C. Behnke. "Women's hostility toward women." *Psychology of Women Quarterly* 22 (1998) 267–284. A woman's hostility toward another woman is correlated with the fact that she doesn't feel good about herself. She has "lower personal self-esteem, optimism, sense of self-efficacy, life satisfaction, and higher objectified body consciousness compared to women who are not hostile toward women;" Adler, Patricia and Peter Adler. "Dynamics of Inclusion and Exclusion in Preadolescent Cliques," *Social Psychology Quarterly* 58 (1995): 156. "Anyone who could create a taunt was favored with attention and imitated by everyone else. Even outsiders who normally were not privileged to pick on a clique member could elevate themselves by joining such taunting. The ultimate degradation was physical;" Simmons, Rachel. *Odd Girl Out: The Hidden Culture of Aggression in Girls.* New York: Harcourt, 2002, p.201. "That the girls who engage in direct conflict may have little real social power is a sad irony, to say the least. The assertiveness shown by some minority girls may reflect not self-confidence but their vulnerability in the larger society. Their voices indeed challenge the picture of indirect aggression … Yet in many instances their forthrightness stems from the girls' sense that they can only make themselves heard by using physical force or dangerous speech. Because it is linked to their marginalization, their directness cannot serve as a model for overcoming girls' sense of powerlessness."

68. Wiseman, Rosalind. *Queen Bee Moms and Kingpin Dads: Dealing with the Parents, Teachers, Coaches, and Counselors who can make—or Break—Your Child's Future.* New York: Crown, 2006, p.170. When school administrators use the excuse that they need more proof before being able to take action against harassment, it sends the message to students that bullying is acceptable as long as they don't get caught.

69. Cohn, Andrea and Andrea Canter National Association of School Psychologists. "Bullying Prevention: What Teachers and Parents Can Do." 7 Oct. 2003. naspcenter.org/factsheets/bullying_fs.html. "Over two-thirds of students believe that schools respond poorly to bullying, with a high percentage of students believing that adult help is infrequent and ineffective."

70. Garbarino, James and Ellen deLara. *And Words Can Hurt Forever: How to Protect Adolescents from Bullying, Harassment, and Emotional Violence.* New York: The Free Press, 2002, p.152, 153, 162.

71. "Lethal Violence in Schools: Can We Prevent School Shootings?" Alfred University. http://www.alfred.edu/teenviolence/canweprevent.html. Crawford, Nicole. "New Ways to Stop Bullying." *American Psychological Association* 33 (2002): 64. "Bullying occurs ... with little variation between urban and suburban towns and rural areas;" Davidson, Tish. *School Conflict.* New York: Scholastic, 2003, p.54.

72. Merten, Don E. "The Meaning of Meanness: Popularity, Competition, and Conflict Among Junior High School Girls." *Sociology of Education* 70 (1997): 183. "School philosophy, which emphasized the need for students to be more independent and self-reliant, dictated that these girls should take care of such conflicts without adult intervention."

73. Garbarino, James and Ellen deLara. *And Words Can Hurt Forever: How to Protect Adolescents from Bullying, Harassment, and Emotional Violence.* New York: The Free Press, 2002, p.15, 84, 120. "Approximately one-third of the students admitted that they had approached an adult in the [school] building with what they considered to be a serious concern, but they were not "listened to" or "taken seriously," and that "nothing had changed as a result of their attempts." School systems are extremely slow to change, and because of this there is a "critical breakdown in any attempt to build a systematic solution to enhance safety and reduce violence."

74. Simmons, Rachel. *Odd Girl Out: The Hidden Culture of Aggression in Girls.* New York: Harcourt, 2002, p.48.

75. Cyberbullying refers to the use of electronic communication such as e-mailing, text-messaging, web blogging, and personal web sites as means to harass, threaten, and alienate an individual; www.cyberbullying.org.

76. Merten, Don E. "The Meaning of Meanness: Popularity, Competition, and Conflict Among Junior High School Girls." *Sociology of Education* 70 (1997): 188. "Popular girls enhanced their chances for continued popularity by being nice" and "treating everyone as an equal."

77. Owens, Lawrence, Rosalyn Shute, and Phillip Slee. "'Guess what I just heard!' Indirect aggression among teenage girls in Australia." *Aggressive Behavior* 26 (2000): 67–83. Girls enlist the help of boys or adults in hurting other girls.

78. Merten, Don E. "The Meaning of Meanness: Popularity, Competition, and Conflict Among Junior High School Girls." *Sociology of Education* 70 (1997): 176, 187–189. "Girls were discouraged from acknowledging their competition even when competition for popularity was pervasive." It's a common cultural dilemma for girls to seek out popularity, but pretend they aren't popular when they reach that success. It's when a girl enjoys her popularity that she's most likely to be called "stuck-up."

79. Crawford, Nicole. "New Ways to Stop Bullying." *American Psychological Association* 33 (2002): 64. "Bullies are more likely to smoke and drink alcohol."

80. Garbarino, James and Ellen deLara. *And Words Can Hurt Forever: How to Protect Adolescents from Bullying, Harassment, and Emotional Violence.* New York: The Free Press, 2002, p.80. "Shaming someone involves a loss of face, diminished self-esteem, and induces a sense of rage."

81. Ibid. p.123. "Some children are scapegoated or stigmatized based on physical attributes, specific mannerisms, or ways they behave. These scapegoats are often the people in the system who are most sensitive to what is going on. Systems utilize scapegoats as a means to resist change; if there is someone to blame, then no one has to look to himself or herself for personal change to make things better."

82. Lawrence Owens, Rosalyn Shute, and Phillip Slee. "'Guess what I just heard!' Indirect aggression among teenage girls in Australia." *Aggressive Behavior* 26 (2000): "This is known as the Provocative Victim explanation."

83. Campbell, Anne. *Men, Women, and Aggression: From Rage in Marriage to Violence in the Streets—How Gender Affects the Way We Act.* New York: Basic Books, 1993, p.18, 50, 56. "When a woman does reach the limit of her self-control and strikes out, [people] tend to be dumbstruck. Her behavior does not fit the representation of coercion and power through which they view it and thus seems unpredictable and pointless." Female aggression, "unlike men's, is not directly aimed at establishing physical victory. Women explode as a means of release. For her, physical aggression is about losing, not winning." Women often erupt when they're fed-up with being manipulated or humiliated by superior peers.

84. Garbarino, James and Ellen deLara. *And Words Can Hurt Forever: How to Protect Adolescents from Bullying, Harassment, and Emotional Violence.* New York: The Free Press, 2002, p.142; Adler, Patricia and Peter Adler. "Dynamics of Inclusion and Exclusion in Preadolescent Cliques," *Social Psychology Quarterly* 58 (1995): 155–156.

85. Chesler, Phillis. *Woman's Inhumanity to Woman.* New York: Thunder's Mouth Press, 2000, p.38. "Women who physically fight other women—or men—are viewed as having "no class.""

86. Tracy, Laura. *The Secret Between Us: Competition Among Women.* Boston: Little, Brown, and Company, 1991, p.14; Ulanov, Ann and Barry. *Cinderella and Her Sisters: The Envied and the Envying.* Hull, Quebec: Daimon, 1998. Envy, which signals our want for sameness, not for separation, undermines our foundations and can become so harmful that it can destroy an entire community.

87. Wiseman, Rosalind. *Queen Bee Moms and Kingpin Dads: Dealing with the Parents, Teachers, Coaches, and Counselors who can make—or Break—Your Child's Future.* New York: Crown, 2006, p.27. "Cultural rule breakers can make others extremely uncomfortable, so most people don't want to be around them. These people seen as "other," possibly tolerated but rarely accepted. Very often, rule breakers aren't respected, their opinions and expe-

riences are easily dismissed, and other people don't want to be seen as associated with them, even when they think the rule breakers are right."

88. Campbell, Anne. *Men, Women, and Aggression: From Rage in Marriage to Violence in the Streets—How Gender Affects the Way We Act.* New York: Basic Books, 1993, p.67. Female aggression is almost always a no-win situation; Evans, Gail. *Play Like a Man, Win Like a Woman: What Men Know About Success That Women Need to Learn.* New York: Broadway Books, 2000, p.67. Women tend to personalize rejection.

89. Wiseman, Rosalind. *Queen Bee Moms and Kingpin Dads: Dealing with the Parents, Teachers, Coaches, and Counselors who can make—or Break—Your Child's Future.* New York: Crown, 2006, p.187. "One of the trademarks of a bad [school official] is that when a student has been bullied, the [school official] "punishes" the perpetrators by making the victim change classes, change schedules, or stay in the office at free periods or recess. A good [school official] will check to see if the victim needs or wants to change his or her schedule, but will also see to it that the perpetrators are the ones who are separated from the group."

90. Adler, Patricia and Peter Adler. "Dynamics of Inclusion and Exclusion in Preadolescent Cliques," *Social Psychology Quarterly* 58 (1995): 145–161.

91. "Some Things You Should Know About Preventing Teen Suicide." American Academy of Pediatrics. http://www.aap.org/advocacy/childhealthmonth/prevteensuicide.htm. Suicide is the third leading cause of death for young people ages 15 to 24. Sixty percent of high school students said they considered suicide, and approximately nine percent said they attempted it at least once; *The AAUW Report: How Schools Shortchange Girls.* Washington, DC: The American Association of University Women Educational Foundation and National Educational Association, 1992, p.79. Adolescent girls are more susceptible to depression and are four times more likely than boys to attempt suicide; "MHAFC Children's Conference to Address Adolescent Depression/TADS Findings." In *Advocate*, a publication of the Mental Health Association of Franklin County. Summer 2006. Columbus, Ohio, p.1. "The occurrence of depression in adolescents has steadily increased over the past ten years. NIMH statistics indicate that one in twenty teens (5%) has moderately severe to severe major depression. Suicide has become the

third leading cause of death in 15 to 24 year olds and the fourth leading cause in 10 to 14 year olds.

92. 1 Corinthians 3:16–17. "Don't you know that you yourselves are God's temple and that God's Spirit lives in you? If anyone destroys God's temple, God will destroy him; for God's temple is sacred, and you are that temple."

93. http://stopbullyingnow.hrsa.gov/index.asp?area=effects.

94. Fillion, Kate. *Lip Service: The Truth About Women's Darker Side in Love, Sex, and Friendship*. New York: Harper Collins, 1996, p.58.

95. Simmons, Rachel. *Odd Girl Out: The Hidden Culture of Aggression in Girls*. New York: Harcourt, 2002, p.78. When girls target another girl, they often downplay their aggression by saying they are just joking.

96. Chelser, Phillis. *Woman's Inhumanity to Woman*. New York: Thunder's Mouth Press, 2000, p.81; Simmons, Rachel. *Odd Girl Out: The Hidden Culture of Aggression in Girls*. New York: Harcourt, 2002, p.82. Victims often feel helpless.

97. Simmons, Rachel. *Odd Girl Out: The Hidden Culture of Aggression in Girls*. New York: Harcourt, 2002, p.127. "As we push girls harder and expect more, girlhood's codes will continue to divide them from one another. These codes have confused, shifted meanings. They are built on a second layer of truth hidden beneath a deceptive exterior. They leave girls ever suspicious of what is really being said and who will be branded next, leaving deep fissures of trust between them ... Friendships are corroded in the silence that is a weak substitute for what must be expressed, for what is real and human and yet feels so sinful. Girlhood's stigma against competition and desire can never allow girls a healthy outlet for their feelings or the kind of straightforward truth telling to which every human being is entitled."

98. 1 Thessalonians 5:17. "Pray continually."

99. Matthew 26: 3–4. "The chief priests and the elders of the people assembled in the palace of the high priest, whose name was Caiaphas, and they plotted to arrest Jesus in some sly way and kill him;" Matthew 26:14–16, 48–49. These passages refer to the betrayal of Jesus by his disciple, Judas; Matthew 26:65–75. This passage refers to Caiaphas' naming Jesus a blasphemer,

which led to the Sanhedrin's verbal and physical attack against Jesus. "They spit in his face and struck him with their fists. Others slapped him and said, "Prophesy to us, Christ. Who hit you?;" Matthew 27:27–31. "Then the governor's soldiers took Jesus into the Praetorium and gathered the whole company of soldiers around him. They stripped him and put a scarlet robe on him, and then twisted together a crown of thorns and set it on his head. They put a staff in his right hand and knelt in front of him and mocked him. "Hail, king of the Jews!" they said. They spit on him, and took the staff and struck him on the head again and again. After they had mocked him, they took off the robe and put his own clothes on him. Then they led him away to crucify him." Matthew 27:37–44. "Above his head they placed the written charge against him: This is Jesus, The King of the Jews. Two robbers were crucified with him, one on his right and one on his left. Those who passed by hurled insults at him, shaking their heads and saying, "You who are going to destroy the temple and build it in three days, save yourself! Come down from the cross, if you are the Son of God!"

In the same way the chief priests, the teachers of the law and the elders mocked him. "He saved others," they said, "but he can't save himself! He's the King of Israel! Let him come down now from the cross, and we will believe in him. He trusts in God. Let God rescue him now if he wants him, for he said, 'I am the Son of God.'" In the same way the robbers who were crucified with him also heaped insults on him;" Luke 4:28–30. This passage refers to Jesus being rejected in Nazareth. The people, angry by his teaching, forced him out of the city and intended to throw him off a cliff, but he "walked right through the crowd and went on his way;" John 6:66. "From this time many of his disciples turned back and no longer followed him."

100. Luke 23:34. "Jesus said, "Father, forgive them, for they do not know what they are doing."

101. 1 Peter 2:24–25. "He himself bore our sins in his body on the tree, so that we might die to sins and live for righteousness; by his wounds you have been healed. For you were like sheep going astray, but now you have returned to the Shepherd and Overseer of your souls."

102. Matthew 6:34. "Therefore do not worry about tomorrow, for tomorrow will worry about itself. Each day has enough trouble of its own."

103. Hebrews 9:28. "… So Christ was sacrificed once to take away the sins of many people; and he will appear a second time, not to bear sin, but to bring salvation to those who are waiting for him."

104. Genesis 37. Joseph's brothers hated him because he was greatly admired by his father and by all of Israel. When Joseph shared his dreams, which predicted his future reign, his brothers became furious and formed an alliance against him. One day, when Joseph went to the fields to find his brothers, he was mocked and attacked. His brothers said, "Here comes the dreamer!" and they plotted to kill him. Reuben talked his brothers out of killing Joseph. Still, they proceeded to strip Joseph of his robe and throw him into an empty cistern. Then they sold him for twenty shekels of silver to the Ishmaelites.

105. Numbers 12. As Moses grew more and more successful, his brother, Aaron, and his sister, Miriam, grew jealous, and they began to badmouth him, primarily because of his foreign wife. Miriam most likely became bitter because she played an important leadership role alongside Moses. She and Aaron not only began complaining about Moses' wife but also their spiritual status in comparison to their brother's. God quickly pointed out to Miriam and Aaron His disapproval of jealousy.

106. Judges 16. Samson's lover, Delilah, was bribed by Samson's enemies, the Philistines, to lure him into revealing the secret of his great strength (his hair) and how he could be overpowered. Delilah manipulated Samson, saying that if he really loved her he would tell her his secret. When he finally told her, she waited until he fell asleep, then she allowed his hair to be shaved off. His strength left him and he was captured by the Philistines, who gouged out his eyes and threw him in prison.

107. 1 Samuel 18–31. David was a respected, victorious warrior. King Saul began to get jealous when Jonathan, Saul's son, developed a strong friendship with David. Even so, Saul promoted David to a high rank in the army because it pleased the people. David went on to be triumphant. The people praised him and favored him to Saul. This infuriated Saul, making him fearful of losing his reign. Thus, he began plotting against David. Saul then tried to set-up a plan in which David would be killed by the Philistines. When this didn't pan-out, Saul advised all of his attendants and Jonathan to kill David.

Saul even tried to kill David on two different occasions, but David escaped. Saul's jealousy and plotting sent David fleeing for his life.

108. Nehemiah 2:19, 4:1–8, 6. When Nehemiah planned to rebuild Jerusalem's wall, Sanballat and Tobiah (two influential politicians) with Geshem, mocked and ridiculed Nehemiah and the Jews. They called the Jews weak and bashed their religion. The rebuilding went forth successfully, which only made Sanballat, Tobiah, and Geshem angrier. They plotted to stir trouble and fight against Jerusalem. The men even sent Nehemiah letters, asking for a casual meeting with him but intending to intimidate and hurt him. Plus, they sent a false prophet, hoping the man would intimidate Nehemiah so that he would sin and they could give him a bad name and ruin his reputation.

109. Acts 6–7. Stephen, "a man full of God's grace and power, did great wonders and miraculous signs among the people." However, members of the Synagogue of the Freedmen and Jews of Alexandria and Cyrene opposed his messages and actions. They argued with him, but Stephen always won, and, of course, the men grew angrier. Then the men secretly persuaded other men to say that Stephen was a blasphemer, and this got everyone gossiping about Stephen and falsely accusing him. So, Stephen was brought in front of the Sanhedrin, where he delivered a courageous speech in defense of Christ that made everyone so angry that they dragged him outside and stoned him to death.

110. Acts 16:19–23. When in the Roman colony of Philippi, a slave girl, who worked as a fortune-teller, began following Paul and Silas for days. She kept yelling, "These men are servants of the Most High God, who are telling you the way to be saved." Paul became so troubled by her that he demanded the evil spirit come out of her. When the spirit left the girl, her owners realized they had just lost a source of income. They seized Paul and Silas, took them to the officials, and accused them of acting unlawfully. A crowd joined in the owner's attack, and without question or trial, Paul and Silas, who were also Roman citizens, were stripped, beaten, and thrown in prison; Acts 17:5–9, 32. After Paul and Silas got out of prison they went to preach in Thessalonica. There, other Jews became jealous, so they "rounded up some bad characters," created a mob, and started a riot. The mob went after Paul and Silas, calling them trouble-makers; Acts 18:6, 12–13; In Corinth, the Jews became abusive and united against Paul; Acts 19:23–41. In Ephesus a

relationally aggressive crowd, led by a silversmith named Demetrius, who was angry that his business would lose money and possibly be destroyed, gathered against Paul Acts 20:3. Just as Paul was about to journey to Syria, the Jews plotted against him again; Acts 21–24. In Jerusalem, the Jews stirred their people and convinced them that Paul was against them and that he was there to destroy them. Paul was seized and the mob tried to kill him. Because Paul held different views, the people shouted, "Rid the earth of him! He's not fit to live!" In speaking before the entire Sanhedrin about the accusations made against him, Paul aroused severe uproar and opposition. As a result, an alliance of 40 conspirators formed against him with the intent to kill him.

111. 1 Peter 5:7. "Cast all your anxiety on him because he cares for you;" Psalm 110:1. "Sit at my right hand until I make your enemies a footstool for your feet;" Zephaniah 3:19. "At that time I will deal with all who oppressed you;" Romans 12:19. "Do not take revenge, my friends, but leave room for God's wrath, for it is written: "It is mine to avenge; I will repay," says the Lord; 1 Peter 1:13. "Therefore, prepare your minds for action; be self-controlled; set your hope fully on the grace to be given you when Jesus Christ is revealed;" Luke 6:27–36. "But I tell you who hear me: Love your enemies, do good to those who hate you, bless those who curse you, pray for those who mistreat you. If someone strikes you on one cheek, turn to him the other also. If someone takes your cloak, do not stop him from taking your tunic. Give to everyone who asks you, and if anyone takes what belongs to you, do not demand it back. Do to others as you would have them do to you.

If you love those who love you, what credit is that to you? Even 'sinners' love those who love them. And if you do good to those who are good to you, what credit is that to you? Even 'sinners' do that. And if you lend to those from whom you expect repayment, what credit is that to you? Even 'sinners' lend to 'sinners,' expecting to be repaid in full. But love your enemies, do good to them, and lend to them without expecting to get anything back. Then your reward will be great, and you will be sons [and daughters] of the Most High, because he is kind to the ungrateful and wicked. Be merciful, just as your Father is merciful; Romans 14:19. "Let us therefore make every effort to do what leads to peace and to mutual edification;" Galatians 5:22–26. "But the fruit of the Spirit is love, joy, peace, patience, kindness, goodness, faithfulness, gentleness and self-control ... Let us not be conceited, provoking and envying each other;" 1 Thessalonians 5:11. "Therefore encourage one another and build each other up;" 2 Timothy 2:22–26. "Flee the evil desires of youth, and pursue righteousness, faith, love and peace, along with those who call on the Lord out of a pure heart. Don't have anything to do with foolish and stupid arguments, because you know they produce quarrels. And the Lord's servant must not quarrel; instead, [she] must be kind to everyone, able to teach, not resentful. Those who oppose him must gently instruct, in the hope that God will grant them repentance leading them to a knowledge of truth, and that they will come to their sense and escape from the trap of the devil, who has taken them captive to do his will; 2 Timothy 4:2. "Preach the Word; be prepared in season and out of season; correct, rebuke and encourage—with great patience and careful instruction;" Titus 3:2. "Remind the people to be subject to rulers and authorities, to be obedient, to be ready to do whatever is good, to slander no one, to be peaceable and considerate, and to show true humility toward all men [and women];" Hebrews 3:13. "But encourage one another daily, as long as it is called Today, so that none of you will be hardened by sin's deceitfulness;" Hebrews 10:25. "Let us not give up meeting together, as some are in the habit of doing, but let us encourage one another—and all the more as you see the Day approaching;" Hebrews 12:14–15. "Make every effort to live in peace with all men and be holy, without holiness no one will see the Lord. See to it that no one misses the grace of God and that no bitter root grows up to cause trouble and defile many;" 1 Peter 3:8–9. "Finally, all of you, live in harmony with one another; be sympathetic, love as brothers [and sisters], be compassionate and humble;" 1 John 3:11–24. "This is the message you heard from the beginning: We should love one another. Do not be like Cain, who belonged to the evil one and murdered his brother. And why did he murder him? Because his own actions were evil and his brother's were righteous. Do not be surprised, my brothers [and sisters], if the world hates you. We know that we have passed from death to life, because we love our brothers [and sisters]. Anyone who does not love remains in death. Anyone who hates his brother [or sister] is a murderer, and you know that no murderer has eternal life in him.

This is how we know what love is: Jesus Christ laid down his life for us. And we ought to lay down our lives for our brothers [and sisters]. If anyone has material possessions and sees his brother in need but has no pity on him, how can the love of God be in him? Dear children, let us not love with words or tongue but with actions and in truth. This then is how we know we belong to the truth, and how we set our hearts at rest in his presence whenever our hearts condemn us. For God is greater than our hearts, and he knows everything. Dear friends, if our hearts do not condemn us, we have confidence before God and receive from him anything we ask, because we obey his commands and do what pleases him. And this is his command: to believe in the name of his Son, Jesus Christ, and to love one another as he commanded us. Those who obey his commands live in him, and he in them. And this is how we know that he lives in us: We know it by the Spirit he gave us."

112. Eichenbaum, Luise and Susie Orbach. *Between Women: Love, Envy, and Competition in Women's Friendships.* New York: Penguin Books, 1987, p.94–95. When the economic, professional, or social synchronicity of women's friendships becomes disturbed, it can be threatening and thus result in relationally aggressive behaviors.

113. Dittmann, Melissa. "Anger across the gender divide: Researchers strive to understand how men and women experience and express anger." *American Psychological Association* 34 (2003): 52. When women are angry they tend to write off people, intending to never speak to them again.

114. Matthew 28:20. "… And surely I am with you always, to the very end of the age."

115. John 16:13. "But when he, the Spirit of all truth, comes, he will guide you into all truth. He will not speak on his own; he will speak only what he hears, and he will tell you what is yet to come."

116. Barash, Susan Shapiro. *Tripping the Prom Queen: The Truth About Women and Rivalry.* New York: St. Martin's Press, 2006; Chesler, Phyllis. *Woman's Inhumanity to Woman.* Thunder Mouth Press: New York, 2001, p.347. When another girl or woman attempts to succeed at something, other females may hold that against her.

117. Ibid. p.5. "But, as men do, women either idealize or demonize women. Most women unconsciously expect other women to mother them and feel betrayed when a woman fails to meet their ideal standards."

118. Goldenbeld, Charles and Jacob M. Rabbie. "Effects of modeling and norm setting on aggressive behavior of males and females." Paper presented at the 6th European Conference of the International Society for Research of

Aggression (ISRA), Jerusalem, Israel, 23–28 June, 1991. In Chesler's *Woman's Inhumanity to Woman,* p.127. "Women are more aggressive in groups than when they are alone and are more easily influenced than men are to punish an opponent who has been programmed to violate a group norm."

119. Isobe M., de Carvalho Filho MK, Maeda K. "Behavioral orientations and peer-contact patterns of relationally aggressive girls." *Psychological Report* 94 (2004): 327–34. "Relationally aggressive groups spent more time engaged in social conversation."

120. Wiseman, Rosalind. *Queen Bee Moms and Kingpin Dads: Dealing with the Parents, Teachers, Coaches, and Counselors who can make—or Break—Your Child's Future.* New York: Crown, 2006, p.137. There are several unwritten rules that guide most girls' anger. The first is that "they sit on it forever, never tell the other person they're mad, and then turn their anger against themselves." The second is that "they sit on it almost forever." They work up the nerve to ask for abuse to stop only to have the other person respond with, "you're being uptight or oversensitive," or, "I'm just being sarcastic." The third is that "they sit on it until something inconsequential sets them off then they explode and the other person dismisses them in the same way." And the fourth is that "they develop a you have no idea who you're dealing with and I will take you down stance," and they fight, either physically, socially, or psychologically, with the other person.

121. Campbell, Anne. *Men, Women, and Aggression: From Rage in Marriage to Violence in the Streets—How Gender Affects the Way We Act.* New York: Basic Books, 1993, p.26. "A major impact of gender identity for girls is the suppression of their own aggression." Being direct is associated with maleness, and females are required to act in an opposite manner; Gail Evans. *Play Like a Man, Win Like a Woman: What Men Know About Success That Women Need to Learn.* Broadway Books, New York: 2000, p.129–131, 148–151.

122. Chesler, Phyllis. *Woman's Inhumanity to Woman.* Thunder Mouth Press: New York, 2001, p.5.

123. Gail Evans. *Play Like a Man, Win Like a Woman: What Men Know About Success That Women Need to Learn.* Broadway Books, New York: 2000, p.129–131, 148–151.

124. Linder, Jennifer, Nicki Crick, and Andrew Collins. "Relational Aggression and Victimization in Young Adults' Romantic Relationships." *Social Development* 11 (2002): 81. "Individuals who are victims of relational aggression are less likely to turn to [the people involved in their life] in times of victimization and instead deal with their needs on their own."

125. Meyer, Joyce. *Beauty to Ashes: Receiving Emotional Healing.* New York: Warner Faith, 2003, p. 131. Fear causes us to hide things; Romans 8:26–27. "The Spirit helps us in our weakness. We do not know what we ought to pray for, but the Spirit himself intercedes for us with groans that words cannot express. And he who searches our hearts knows the mind of the Spirit, because the Spirit intercedes for the saints in accordance with God's will."

126. Jeremiah 31:34. "For I will forgive their wickedness and will remember their sins no more."

127. Romans 12:21. "Do not be overcome by evil, but overcome evil with good."

128. Dittman, Melissa. "Anger across the gender division: Researchers strive to understand how men and women experience and express anger." *American Psychological Association* 34 (2003): 52. Women tend to write each other off.

129. Luke 23:34.

130. 1 John 2:9–12. "Anyone who claims to be in the light but hates [her sister and brother] is still in the darkness. Whoever loves [her sister and brother] lives in the light, and there is nothing in [her] to make [her] stumble. But whoever hates [her sister or brother] is in the darkness and walks around in the darkness; [she] does not know where [she] is going, because the darkness has blinded [her]."

131. Meyer, Joyce. *Beauty to Ashes: Receiving Emotional Healing.* New York: Warner Faith, 2003; O'Neill, Jennifer. *From Fallen to Forgiven: A Spiritual Journey into Wholeness and Healing.* Nashville: W Publishing Group, 2001.

132. Barash, Susan Shapiro. *Tripping the Prom Queen: The Truth About Women and Rivalry.* New York: St. Martin's Press, 2006, p.118, 131.

133. Gushee, David P. "Many balk at forgiveness, but it's essential." *The Columbus Dispatch*, 21 May, 2004: E2.

134. Fillion, Kate. *Lip Service: The Truth About Women's Darker Side in Love, Sex, and Friendship.* New York: Harper Collins, 1996, p.61, 75.

135. Mooney, Nan. *I Can't Believe She Did That! Why Women Betray Other Women at Work.* New York: St. Martin's Press, 2005, p.189.

136. Gilligan, Carol. *In a Different Voice.* Cambridge: Harvard University Press, 1982, p.8.

137. Fillion, Kate. *Lip Service: The Truth About Women's Darker Side in Love, Sex, and Friendship.* New York: Harper Collins, 1996, p.61, 76.

138. Chesler, Phyllis. *Woman's Inhumanity to Woman.* Thunder Mouth Press: New York, 2001.

139. Brown, Lyn Mikel. "Cultivating Hardiness Zones for Adolescent Girls." Paper presented at the Girls' Health Summit. 1 June 2001. "Girls need experiences in which they exert control over more than their bodies, sexuality or appearance; where they can connect to their own worth, to a positive belief system and to others who will commit to them, and where they can experience support and encouragement to learn and persist in the face of struggles;" Pipher, Mary. Reviving Ophelia: *Saving the Selves of Adolescent Girls.* New York: Ballantine, 1994, p.283, 284. "In order to keep to their true selves and grow into healthy adults, girls need love from family and friends, meaningful work, respect, challenges and physical and psychological safety. They need identities based on talents and interests rather than appearance, popularity or sexuality. They need good habits for coping with stress, self-nurturing skills and a sense of purpose and perspective. They need quiet places and times. They need to feel that they are part of something larger than their own lives and that they are emotionally connected to a whole;" Galatians 3:26–29. "You all are sons [and daughters] of God through faith in Christ Jesus, for all of you who were baptized into Christ have clothed yourselves with Christ. There is neither Jew nor Greek, slave

nor free, male nor female, for you are all one in Christ Jesus. If you belong to Christ, then you are Abraham's seed, and heirs according to the promise."

140. Mooney, Nan. *I Can't Believe She Did That! Why Women Betray Other Women at Work*. New York: St. Martin's Press, 2005, p.171.

141. Galatians 6: 7–8. "Do not be deceived: God cannot be mocked."

Acknowledgements

I spent about three years writing this book, often feeling as if I were trailing behind "normal" life, but I always knew I was supposed to do this, no matter what I had to sacrifice. I thank God and my family for knowing that I was supposed to write this book too. I am thankful to Mom, Dad, and Mattie for their patience, because, for over two years, I wouldn't even let them read my writing. Thank you, my family, for taking care of me when I couldn't take care of myself. Thank you, Charlie, for all of the times that I asked, "Would you please read this," and you gladly accepted. I also thank you for being understanding and patient as I put "things" on hold.

Nancy Mcdonald-Kenworthy and Nick Scorza, both of you saved me major bucks in editing! Thank you. Sarah Smith at Kent Smith Photography, I pray that the Holy Spirit keeps moving through your studio. My brothers in Christ, Pillar, I'm thankful that Kalel asked me, "Is there another calf raise machine in here?" Your music continues to give me the direction I need in times of big decision.

Thank you, Dan Stasiewski of The Ophelia Project for your diligence and for leading me to Ophelia's founder, Susan Wellman. Susan, your words were so uplifting, and I look forward to uniting with you and other leaders of The Ophelia Project to combat relational aggression. Thank you, Brenda High of Bully Police USA, for using Jared's tragic story to touch so many peoples' lives and launch an effort that has already made a huge impact worldwide. Elizabeth Bennett, I wish you continued success with your book and your fight against Peer Abuse, and I pray God blesses you for being so helpful to me. I appreciate the friends I've made online while promoting my book. Your support and personal stories are inspirational. I'm hopeful your anti-bullying efforts will payoff, and I look forward to growing relationships with all of you. Also, thank you to all of the people who consistently asked my family and me, "When's that book gonna be done?" I appreciate your curiosity and support.

978-0-595-45839-4
0-595-45839-4

Made in the USA
Lexington, KY
12 April 2010